HEALING THE GLOBAL INTIMACY DISORDER

HEALING THE GLOBAL INTIMACY DISORDER

TOWARDS A NEW POLITICS OF EVOLUTIONARY LOVE

A PLANETARY AWAKENING IN LOVE THROUGH UNIQUE SELF SYMPHONY

• • •

From Conscious Evolution 1.0 to Conscious Evolution 2.0

One Mountain, Many Paths: Oral Essays
Volume Two

DR. MARC GAFNI AND BARBARA MARX HUBBARD

Copyright © 2025 Center for World Philosophy and Religion

All Rights Reserved

No part of this book may be used or reproduced in any manner whatsoever without written permission except in the case of brief quotations embodied in critical articles or reviews.

No part of this book may be reproduced, or stored in a retrieval system, or transmitted in any form or by any means, electronic, mechanical, photocopying, recording, or otherwise, without express written permission of the publisher.

All brand names and product names used in this book are trademarks, registered trademarks, or trade names of their respective holders.

For additional information and press releases please contact CWPR Publishing.

Author: Marc Gafni and Barbara Marx Hubbard
Title: Healing the Global Intimacy Disorder
From Conscious Evolution 1.0 to Conscious Evolution 2.0

Identifiers: ISBN 979-8-88834-046-2 (electronic)
ISBN 979-8-88834-045-5 (paperback)

Edited by Kristina Amelong, Timothy Paul Aryeh, Paul Bennett, Carol Herndon, and Rachel Keune

World Philosophy and Religion Press, St. Johnsbury, VT
in conjunction with

IP Integral Publishers

https://worldphilosophyandreligion.org

JOIN THE REVOLUTION!

CONTENTS

EDITORIAL NOTE ABOUT AUTHORSHIP, EDITING, AND THE RADICAL CONTEXT FOR THIS SERIES — XIII

LOVE OR DIE: LOCATING OURSELVES — XXV

ABOUT THIS VOLUME — XLII

CHAPTER 1   CELEBRATING EPIPHANY: THE BIRTH OF THE NEW HUMAN AND THE NEW HUMANITY

Epiphany of Homo Universalis, a New Human — 1
We Are Spiritually Incorrect Evangelicals — 3
Epiphany Is Transcending the Regular — 4
There Is No Compelling Vision of Postmodernity — 5
Can We Open Up to Epiphany? — 7
Evolving Prayer: God, Love Me Open! — 8
Tipping the Scales of Evolution Towards More Life and More Love — 11
Why Is the Universe a Love Story? — 13
The Divine Whisper: Synchronicity — 14

CHAPTER 2   PRINCIPLES OF A PERSONAL POLITICS OF EVOLUTIONARY LOVE

A Politics of Evolutionary Love — 18
Five Core Principles of a Politics of Evolutionary Love — 21
The Strange Attractor Is Unique Self — 26

Meditation: Breathe From the Deep Impulse of
    Evolution Within Us   27

Knowing God as the Greatest Love of Your Life   28

The Infinite Power of Cosmos   30

CHAPTER 3   FROM POWERLESSNESS TO SACRED ACTIVISM

Tuning Into the Impulse of Creation   34

Prayers to the Power of Democracy   35

Reality Yearns for Us   37

It Is Not Your Job to Heal the Whole Thing   43

Why Isn't Everyone Out There Doing It?   44

When We Claim Our Power, We Close the Gap Between
    Our Ability To Heal and Our Ability To Feel   47

Confessing Our Greatness   48

Yom Kippur Story of Yankel   48

CHAPTER 4   EVOLUTION'S DESIRE FOR SYNERGISTIC DEMOCRACY

Awakening a Memory of the Future   52

Finding the Field   53

The Evolutionary God Is the Impulse of Evolution
    and the Beloved Who Holds It All   55

Praying from the Place of the Lonely Child   58

Announcing Synergistic Democracy   59

The Wheel of Co-Creation in Synergistic Democracy   61

The Democratization of Enlightenment: Every Unique Self Is
    Needed by All-That-Is   64

You've Got to Take a Unique Stand   64

Moving Beyond Ordinary Love to Outrageous Love   66

Your Unique Risk Is What Makes You Alive   67

CHAPTER 5   EVOLUTION AND CONNECTION

Feel the Force of Outrageous Love Within	70
God as the Mother Who Nourishes Us	72
Let Evolution Move Forward	73
Imagining the Third Face of God	74
Prayer and Sex Are the Same Thing: You Can't Pretend	76
A Taste of Planetary Connection	77
Evolutionary Love Is Outrageous Love	81
Three Distinctions Between Ordinary Love and Outrageous Love	83
Story: The Great Master of Children	86
Let Us Bring Mass Empathy	90

CHAPTER 6   HEALING THE GLOBAL INTIMACY DISORDER WITH A NEW POLITICS OF INTIMACY

Radical Planetary Intimacy	92
The Missing Tile Syndrome	93
The Scroll of Esther	95
The Intimate Kiss of Prayer	96
Radical Fulfillment of Living Your Heart's Desire	98
What Does Co-Creation Mean?	100
The Exile of Intimacy	102

CHAPTER 7   THE COLLECTIVE AWAKENING OF HUMANITY

Meditation: One Evolutionary Act of Love	107
Restoring Intimacy: God Is Always with Us, and Feeling Every Pulse of Our Interior.	108
The Three Faces of God	109
Offering Prayer to the Infinity of Intimacy	111

Experience a Planetary Birth in Response to Pain	112
The Four Questions to Help Create the Planetary Awakening	117
You Cannot Enter Intimacy Holding Hate in Your Heart	117
The Day of Atonement	118

CHAPTER 8 THE EVOLUTION OF REALITY IS THE EVOLUTION OF LOVE

No One Lives a Life of Lonely Desperation	120
When You Give Your Genuine Gift of Love the Whole Way, the Suffering is Gone	123
What Does Love, or Outrageous Love, Mean at a Higher Level of Consciousness?	128
Our Greatness Is Imbued with the Enormity of the Desire of Evolution for More Life, More Love, More Creativity	131
By Re-Sourcing We Return Deeper to Our Source	132

CHAPTER 9 INTERCONNECTION, INTIMACY, AND A MEMORY OF THE FUTURE

Healing Separation	134
In the Intimate Universe No One Is Left Out of the Circle	135
God of Intimacy	137
This Extraordinary Moment in History	138
The Last Day of the Creation of the Old Is Obviously the First Day of the Creation of the New	139
From Atonement to Attunement	141
We Are the Unique Self Symphony, Together— Let's Feel It Arise	142
The Insane King	143
Hope Is a Memory of the Future	144

CHAPTER 10 BECOMING AGENTS OF INTIMACY FOR A NEW STORY

Innovation on the Inside: You Become the Agent of Intimacy	148
Loneliness on Two Levels	149
Existential Risk	150
In the Face of Existential Risk, We Do Not Have To Do the Whole Thing	151
A New Universe Story Raises All Ships	152
We Hear God in the Deep Small Voice	154
Joining Genius on a Meta Scale	156
When Syncon Sectors Became Connected, It Was a Social Love Affair	157
Reality Is a Story and it is Going Somewhere	160
Hope Is a Memory of the Future	164

INDEX   **172**

EDITORIAL NOTE ABOUT AUTHORSHIP, EDITING, AND THE RADICAL CONTEXT FOR THIS SERIES

ORAL ESSAYS FROM THE ONE MOUNTAIN, MANY PATHS WEEKLY BROADCAST

This volume is part of the Oral Essays library, a series of lightly edited, compiled transcripts of oral teachings given by Dr. Marc Gafni and the late Barbara Marx Hubbard in their weekly online broadcast, *One Mountain, Many Paths*, which they co-founded in 2017. Originally called an "Evolutionary Church," *One Mountain, Many Paths* became a key venue for the articulation of an inspired and deeply grounded new Story of Value in response to the meta-crisis. Marc and Barbara—together with Zak Stein,[1] Kristina Kincaid, Ken Wilber, Sally Kempton, Lori Galperin, Aubrey Marcus and dozens of other thought-leaders over the years—began to articulate what they call a World Philosophy and World Religion[2] as a context for our diversity.

---

1 Zak, together with Ken Wilber, has been Marc's primary intellectual partner and an initiate lineage holder in CosmoErotic Humanism.

2 This project is grounded in four core organizational frameworks: 1) The Center for World Philosophy and Religion, co-founded by Marc Gafni, Zachary Stein, Sally Kempton, and Ken Wilber, and chaired over the years by John P. Mackey, Barbara Marx Hubbard, Aubrey Marcus, Gabrielle Anwar and Shareef Malnik, Carrie Kish and Adam Bellow, and Kathleen J. Brownback. 2) The Office for the Future, chaired by Stephanie Valcke and Ivan Bossyut. 3) The World Philosophy and Religion Press, founded and chaired by Aubrey Marcus, together with Marc Gafni and Zachary Stein. 4) The Foundation for Conscious Evolution, founded by Barbara Marx Hubbard and currently chaired by Peter Fiekowsky. For a complete list of key leadership, see the Office for the Future website, www.officeforthefuture.com.

Until Barbara's passing in 2019, she and Marc transmitted teachings together as evolutionary partners and "whole mates," weaving together insights and transmissions from their decades of practice, study, teaching, and activism into a synergy of wisdom, a grounded vision for future policy across all sectors of society.

Much of the Dharma material below comes directly from Marc, so it was originally all in quotation marks—but that looked a little odd. So per his suggestion we removed them, and the reader should consider the paragraphs on the next several pages as one extended quote from him. We are joyfully grateful to Marc for the clarity of his Dharma, the elegance and "second simplicity" of this language, and the mad, Outrageous Love with which he transmits his teachings.

Barbara and Marc called the mission of *One Mountain* "a Planetary Awakening in Evolutionary Love Through Unique Self Symphonies." We are an evolutionary community with a deeply grounded, radically alive, and "post-tragic" revolutionary spirit. We are activating a new humanity and awakening as a new species: *Homo amor*, the fulfillment of *Homo sapiens*.

One Mountain is committed to articulating a Story of Value that can become the ground for the new society that must be birthed in response to the meta-crisis. We recognize that we are living at a pivotal moment in history. In this "time between stories," the great moral imperative is to tell the new Story of Value. It is ours to do, personally and collectively, with great trembling and ecstatic joy.

FROM DOGMA TO DHARMA: ETERNAL AND EVOLVING FIRST PRINCIPLES AND FIRST VALUES

The teachings are grounded in decades of deep study across many wisdom traditions. Over the years, week by week, these teachings were incrementally developed within the framework of the *One Mountain, Many Paths* broadcast. We often refer to these teachings as *Dharma*.

EDITORIAL NOTE

This word was originally used in lineage traditions to refer to something like universal law. This is a crucial realization: just as there is universal law in mathematical value, there is also a sense of universal law in ethics and value.

Historically, Dharma often devolved into unchanging dogma. Evolution was ignored, and the natural process of Dharma evolution became disconnected from its deep, eternal context. The weakness of the word Dharma is that too often it did not include the evolving insights of the sciences, it confused local cultural truths with universal truths, and it used words like "eternal," as in "eternal Tao," as opposed to words like "evolution."

Eternal came to mean unchanging, and that kind of thinking often led to overly ethnocentric readings of Dharma. Local systems would claim their religious and cultural insights as immutable, which stood in the way of the emergence of a genuine world Story of Value that is real, inherent to Cosmos, and backed by the Universe—even as it is also always evolving.

Or, as we often say, "eternal value is evolving value. The eternal Tao is the evolving Tao."

We have shown that, emergent from profound insights in the "interior sciences," eternal does not mean unchanging in time; it means what we call the deeper Field of ErosValue that is beneath culture, geography, and history, which lives beneath all individual and collective values, and beneath time and space itself.

As such, we have gradually transitioned from the term Dharma to the term *Value*, in the sense of the Field of Value that lives beneath all values. This Field of Value discloses as First Principles and First Values embedded in a Story of Value.

Indeed, as the interior sciences knew and the exterior sciences imply, Reality arises in a Field of ErosValue in which an entire set of mathematical, musical, molecular, moral, and mystical values are the very ground of all being. That Field of Value is eternal—the true ground of the Good, True and Beautiful—even as it is evolving.

But of course, it is equally critical not just to talk about evolving value, but to ground the evolving value in its true nature, the eternal Field of First Principles and First Values, always reaching for ever-more life, ever-more love, ever-more care, ever-more depth, ever-more uniqueness, ever-more intimate communion, and ever-more transformation.

As such, when we refer to the word Dharma, which still appears in these texts together with the word value, we refer to an evolving Dharma grounded in an *eternal and evolving* Field of Value. Indeed, eternity and evolution are two faces of the whole, opposites joined at the hip, that characterize the nature of our Cosmos in virtually all of its expressions.

It's in these terms that we ground a robust world philosophy that integrates the validated, leading-edge insights of premodern traditional wisdom, modern wisdom, and more recent postmodern insights, weaving them together into a new whole greater than the sum of its parts.

This new whole is a shared Story of Value rooted in First Principles and First Values that are both eternal and evolving.

These First Principles and First Values of Cosmos are woven together into a new Story of Value as a context for our diversity, a new Universe Story. This new Story gives us the best possible responses we have to the mystery, and to the great questions:

- Who am I? Who are we?
- Where am I? Where are we?
- What should I do? What should we do?

It is only through such a shared Universe Story—a narrative of identity and ethos as a context for our blessed diversity—that we can realize how what unites is so much greater than what divides us.

EDITORIAL NOTE

Only a new Story of Value will allow us to both respond to the meta-crisis and participate together in birthing the most true, good, and beautiful world that we already know is possible.

THIS ORAL ESSAYS SERIES IS AN ENTRYWAY TO THE GREAT LIBRARY OF COSMOEROTIC HUMANISM

This Oral Essays series is part of the overarching project of the Great Library at the Center for World Philosophy and Religion, led by Dr. Marc Gafni, together with Dr. Zak Stein. The aim of the Great Library project is to articulate a robust and comprehensive new Story of Value, CosmoErotic Humanism, in the form of dozens of well-researched and extensively footnoted academic works.

Our vision is to provide the philosophical framework that will be vital for navigating humanity through this time of immense crisis and transformation.

To begin your journey into CosmoErotic Humanism, we tenderly refer you to the book *First Principles and First Values*, co-authored by Marc Gafni, Zak Stein, and Ken Wilber, under the name David J. Temple. David J. Temple is a pseudonym created for enabling ongoing collaborative authorship at the Center for World Philosophy and Religion. The two primary authors behind David J. Temple are Marc Gafni and Zak Stein, and for different projects, specific writers will be named as part of the collaboration, such as Ken Wilber and others.

Three other volumes complete this introduction: *A Return to Eros*, by Marc Gafni and Kristina Kincaid; *Your Unique Self*, by Marc Gafni; and *Education in a Time between Worlds*, by Zak Stein.

We hope that the Oral Essays in this volume, with their informal style of transmission, will serve as an allurement and entryway for you into the more formal books of the Great Library that provide the robust intellectual underpinnings of the new Story of Value.

A NOTE ABOUT THE EDITORS

This Oral Essays collection has been edited by students of the new Story of CosmoErotic Humanism. Each of us has actively participated in *One Mountain, Many Paths*, and most of us have been in deep "Holy of Holies" study with Dr. Marc Gafni for many years.

We have been privileged to find ourselves well-versed in the teachings, and even emerging as lineage-holders of CosmoErotic Humanism.[3]

We view this editing project as a privilege and a deep practice of study and clarification. We experience ourselves as a *mystical editing society*, frequently meeting and conversing together about the content—the depth of knowledge and wisdom offered here—as well as the technical intricacies involved with publishing a beautiful and coherent series of books. In so doing, we function as a "Unique Self Symphony," which itself is a Dharmic

---

3   CosmoErotic Humanism is a world philosophical movement aimed at reconstructing the collapse of value at the core of global culture. Much like Romanticism or Existentialism, CosmoErotic Humanism is not merely a theory but a movement that changes the very mood of Reality. It is an invitation to participate in evolving the source code of consciousness and culture towards a cosmocentric *ethos* for a planetary civilization.

The term CosmoErotic Humanism, initially coined by Dr. Gafni and colleagues, points to a complex, multi-faceted, layered, and nuanced evolutionary set of insights that has evolved over decades of intensive research, teaching, and spiritual practice from deep within a wide range of wisdom traditions (including the Wisdom of Solomon lineage tradition, Bodhisattva Buddhism, and Kashmir Shaivism), as well as multiple disciplines including complexity theory, chaos theory, emergence theory, molecular biology, and the more classical disciplines of the humanities.

The seeds of CosmoErotic Humanism were planted with Dr. Marc Gafni's work on a two-volume, 1,000-page opus called *Radical Kabbalah* (Integral Publishers, 2012). This scholarly work, sourced from deep study within the esoteric lineage texts of the Wisdom of Solomon, points to a non-dual, or acosmic, realization which—unlike the prevailing conceptualization of non-duality—does not efface the human being; rather, it is highly humanistic in its nature. The next step in the evolution of CosmoErotic Humanism was the insight that all of Reality is evolving Eros, which lives in, as, and through the human being.

A failure of Eros leads inexorably to the creation of narratives of "pseudo-eros." CosmoErotic Humanism is a response to the modern mental and social breakdown sourced in the proliferation of multiple forms of pseudo-eros and its broken narratives, such as rivalrous conflict governed by win/lose metrics and the dogmatic denial of intrinsic value in Cosmos, which together generate our current "global intimacy disorder."

term that connotes an omni-considerate collaboration between realized Unique Selves synergizing our unique gifts into a new emergence greater than the sum of the parts. Even as we worked diligently to standardize our editing styles, meeting on a weekly basis to debate the nuances of phrasing, we also operated from within a deep appreciation of the unique style that each editor brought to his or her work. As such, the reader might notice some variation in editing style among the books.

Please note that Dr. Marc Gafni has not reviewed these edited Oral Essays, as he is deeply engaged in writing the formal books of the Great Library. But he has been generous in responding to questions and providing overall guidance in the project. Overall, as Marc's students and students of the Dharma, we have made it a key project at the Center to publish these pieces of work relatively independently.

OUR UNIQUE ORAL-ESSAY EDITING STYLE PRESERVES THE ENERGY OF THE ORIGINAL TRANSMISSION

Dr. Marc Gafni is a uniquely gifted teacher whose oral transmission is imbued with a quality that has proven transformative for his students. Many of us feel mystically transformed by both the content and the underlying energy of the transmission style. Therefore, as we like to say, *trust the magic ways the Dharma comes through your unique understanding!*

As Marc's empowered students, colleagues, and beloved friends, we have a deep knowing that these teachings are vital for the survival and thriving of humanity as we know it, and we recognize the importance of publishing his teachings in a written format that will be accessible by future generations. At the same time, we sought to preserve the Eros of the original oral transmission with all of its nuance, power, and depth. Our intention in the editing process, to the greatest extent possible, has been to keep these spoken artifacts intact in order to maintain the flow of the original transmission. We have therefore chosen not to engage in intensive formal editing, as we found that doing so resulted in the loss of the energetic transmission that is so key to fully receiving the Dharma.

After experimenting with many ways to present these texts, we developed a specific way of laying out the text on the page. Marc, in collaboration with Zak Stein and Russian intellectual/artist Elena Maslova-Levin—and ultimately all of the editors, through many conversations—developed a unique, artistic presentation of the text, using bolding, italics, bullet points, and other stylistic features which together serve to accentuate the immediacy of the oral transmission.

As part of this editing style, intended to preserve the integrity of the original transmission, we have refrained from removing the frequent recapitulations of key themes. We found that each recapitulation contributes something vital to the rhythm and music beneath the words, like the beating drum of our hearts. These recapitulations not only review previous material but also add important new emphases, perspectives, and elements of the new Story of Value. We ask for your patience as a reader to trust the rhythm of these texts, and we trust you as a reader to have the depth and steadiness to find your way through.

KEY COMPONENTS: LINK TO THE ORIGINAL BROADCAST, EVOLUTIONARY LOVE CODES AND PRAYER

To supplement the written word, each episode includes a QR code linking to the original broadcast on YouTube, as well as occasional links to featured songs and video clips.

Each episode also centers around an "Evolutionary Love Code," formulated by Marc. These codes are part of the ongoing articulation and distillation of the Dharma as it unfolds and emerges, week by week, over the course of many years, through the mystical process we call Outrageous Love or Evolutionary Love.

EDITORIAL NOTE

Another core component of the *One Mountain, Many Paths* episodes is what Marc and Barbara called "Evolutionary Prayer." Prayer is experienced in *One Mountain* not in the old fundamentalist sense of a "cosmic vending-machine god" who is alienated from Cosmos. Marc refers to this as the "god you do not and should not believe in"—and he often adds, "the god you don't believe in does not exist."

GOD IS THE INFINITE INTIMATE

In fact, in the Dharma of CosmoErotic Humanism, a new name for God has emerged: the "Infinite Intimate," who appears in first-, second-, and third-person expressions. Marc first shared this name as he heard it whispered in 2023, although earlier intimations and formulations of the name appeared as early as 2010.

In first person, God is infinitely alive and as intimate as our own first-person experience.

In second person, God is the infinitely intimate Personhood of Cosmos that knows our name and holds us—the God about whom we say, *whenever we fall, we fall into Her hands*. This is the God who is our Beloved, Father, Mother, Lover, and Evolutionary Partner.

Finally, in third person, God inheres in all of the First Principles and First Values of Cosmos, and in the laws of science (both interior and exterior) that govern manifest Reality.

Therefore, we have a realization of God as not only the Infinity of Power but also the Infinity of Intimacy.

In *One Mountain, Many Paths*, we are reclaiming prayer at a higher level of consciousness. And we are reclaiming prayer as deep, alive, loving, and intimate conversations with God as the Infinite Intimate who knows our name.

REFLECTING ON THE CO-CREATION BETWEEN DR. MARC GAFNI AND BARBARA MARX HUBBARD

Barbara and Marc met five years before Barbara passed. As Barbara said so often, "before I met Marc, I was sure that I was done." Barbara had taught so beautifully for decades, focusing particularly on a powerful articulation of "conscious evolution."

Indeed, it would not be inaccurate to say that Barbara was the greatest storyteller of conscious evolution of her time.

Conscious evolution was also a premise in Marc's thinking, but drawn from an entirely different set of sources and experiences. Barbara drew from the classical sources of evolutionary spirituality, such as Teilhard de Chardin, Buckminster Fuller, and many others. Indeed, she was closely associated with Fuller, and was perhaps de Chardin's most ardent intellectual devotee.

Marc drew a somewhat different vision of conscious evolution from the interior sciences of the great wisdom traditions, with a primary emphasis on what he refers to as the "Solomon lineages," merged together with careful readings of the leading edges of the sciences.

In the old version of conscious evolution, the movement from unconscious to conscious was a movement of evolution by chance to evolution by choice.

Together Marc and Barbara evolved the old version of Conscious Evolution, pointing out that evolution itself was always in some sense conscious, but as Marc formulated it, the awakening to conscious evolution refers to the awakening of evolution as human consciousness, coupled with the human realization of being conscious evolution in person, and the human capacity to locate oneself within the context of the larger evolutionary story.

Marc focused his attention on an entirely different dimension of Reality, which he and his colleagues began to call CosmoErotic Humanism.

EDITORIAL NOTE

The Intimate Universe, Homo amor, Unique Self and Unique Self Symphonies, God as the Infinity of Intimacy, Eros and the CosmoErotic Universe, distinctions like Role Mate, Soul Mate and Whole Mate, the Four Selves, Evolutionary Love, Outrageous Love, Evolution: the Love Story of the Universe, First Principles and First Values, Evolving Perennialism, the Evolution of Love, and many more are terms articulated by Gafni and shared with Barbara in their conversation, study, and creative engagement.

Some terms they coined together, for example "a Planetary Awakening in Love through Unique Self Symphonies," where Gafni described Unique Self Symphonies, and Barbara aligned her vision of a planetary Pentecost to Marc's vision of Unique Self Symphonies.

Other key terms were unique and articulated by Barbara, for example: conscious evolution, teleros, telerotic, from joining genes to joining genius, regenopause, vocational arousal, birthing of humanity, synergy engine, and of course her work around what she called the Wheel of Co-creation.

Ultimately, Marc and Barbara attempted to synergize their work in what they called the Wheel of Co-creation 2.0. Barbara and Marc experienced themselves as merging their respective Dharma into what they began to refer to as Conscious Evolution 2.0, or later, CosmoErotic Humanism.

The first 129 episodes of One Mountain, Many Paths took place in the last period of Barbara's life and reflect the depth and texture of the stunning evolutionary whole-mate meeting between her and Marc.

As Barbara was deep in study with Marc, a lot of what she shared in Evolutionary Church was the Dharma of their deep study and collaboration.

Although sometimes it may be clear who is speaking, we generally publish these early episodes in what we are calling "one voice." The first 129 episodes, with Marc and Barbara together, have been grouped chronologically.

Episodes 130 to 400 and onwards, which were transmitted by Marc, have been grouped by topic.

THE INVITATION

We invite you to find your way into this revolution. Each one of our Unique Selves and unique gifts are desperately needed as we co-create this new Story of Value together, as part of the covenant between generations, for the sake of the whole.

Let's *play a larger game* and evolve the very source code of consciousness and culture together.

With mad love,

The Editors

LOVE OR DIE

LOCATING OURSELVES: ARTICULATING THE ESSENTIAL CONTEXT FOR THE ONE MOUNTAIN, MANY PATHS ORAL ESSAYS

SETTING OUR INTENTION

Intention setting is everything.

We're here—as da Vinci was with his cohort in the Renaissance—**to play a larger game, to participate in the evolution of love, which is to tell the new Story of Value rooted in First Principles and First Values.**

- Our intention is to recognize the critical historical juncture in which we find ourselves.
- Our intention is to take our seat at the table of history and to say, *we take responsibility for this.*
- Our intention is to participate as revolutionaries for the sake of the whole.

What we're here to do is revolution; revolution for the sake of the evolution of love.

It's a revolution for the sake of the trillions of unborn lives that will not manifest:

- The unborn loves
- The unborn creativity
- The unborn goodness
- The unborn truth
- The unborn beauty

All of it looks to us.

Not because we're engaged in grandiosity. Not at all!

- We're trembling before She.
- We're trembling with joy at the privilege.
- We're trembling with joy at the responsibility.
- We're trembling with joy at the Possibility of Possibility.
- We have to enact a new Story in this moment of time. Because it is only a new Story that can change the vector of history.

The most revolutionary act that we can do—the greatest moral imperative of this time—**is to articulate a new Story at this time between worlds and this time between stories.**

Story is not made up, as postmodernity suggests. **We all live in inescapable frameworks; our framework is the story we live in.** Right now, Reality lives according to win/lose metrics, a story that is generating existential risk. **We need to change that story.**

When we change that story, when we tell a new Story—not a made-up story, but a new Story of Value, rooted in First Principles and First Values—**then it all changes.**

We need to participate in the evolution of the source code of consciousness and culture, which is the evolution of love.

It's the most important, exciting, evolutionary, revolutionary act that we can do to alleviate suffering: to be lovers.

Like Rumi, the great poet of Sufism, we have to be "mad lovers," because it's the only sanity.

To be mad lovers is to see around the corner, to not be so obsessed with the details of the contractions of my life.

Let me see bigger.

Let me take complete care of myself in every possible way, let me completely attend to those in my circle of intimacy and influence, and then—*let me expand my circle.*

That's what we're here for.

- Our intention is to participate in the *LoveForce*, the *LoveIntelligence*, the *LoveBeauty*, the *LoveDesire* that literally animates Cosmos all the way up and all the way down.
- Our intention is to participate in the evolution of love.

> [*In the next few pages we will cover some key concepts which are essential to locating ourselves and setting the context for all the One Mountain, Many Paths Oral Essays. —Eds.*]

OVERVIEW: EROS IS NO LONGER A LUXURY—IT'S LOVE OR DIE

Eros is life.

The failure of Eros destroys life.

Our lack of Eros is poised to destroy the world.

All civilizations have fallen because the stories that they lived in were, in some sense, stories based on rivalrous conflict governed by win/lose metrics. Every civilization was weakened by interior polarization caused by the lack of a shared Story of Value.

We now have a global civilization, but we haven't created a shared Story of Value.

We haven't solved the generator functions that caused all civilizations to fall. Our global civilization has exponential technologies and extraction models depleting the Earth of resources that took billions of years to create, which is going to lead to a civilizational collapse.

Existential risk is risk to our very existence.

The choice is clear: love or die.

It's that simple.

Eros is no longer a luxury. It is an absolute necessity for the survival of the individual and the planet.

In the last half a century, modern psychology has documented an age-old truth: a fully nourished baby who is not held in loving arms will die.

So too, our world, both personal and global—even with all the resources of intelligence and technology at our disposal—will die without being held in love, in the embrace of Eros.

We must embrace a personal path of love and a global politics of love.

Not ordinary love. Not love which is "mere human sentiment," but Eros, or what we sometimes call Outrageous Love, which is the heart of existence itself.

We live in a world of outrageous pain.

The only response is Outrageous Love.

WHAT IS EROS?

Eros is the experience of radical aliveness, moving towards, seeking, desiring ever-deeper contact and ever-greater wholeness.[4] Eros is the core fabric of Reality's being and the motivational architecture of Reality's becoming.

Eros is what animates the evolutionary impulse itself, from the very inception of Cosmos all the way to our very selves, who awaken to the realization that the evolutionary impulse throbs uniquely in each of us.

The realization of human awakening and transformation that lies at the core of the interior sciences is the invitation—or even the urgent and desperate demand—of a madly loving Cosmos animated by infinities of power and infinities of intimacy.

The demand—the desperate invitation, the plea, the tender and fierce command of Cosmos that lives inside every human being—is to awaken: to awaken to our true nature as unique incarnations of Eros and Ethos that are needed and desperately desired by All-That-Is. Said slightly differently: Reality is Eros. Or: God is Eros.

The failure of Eros destroys life. The collapse of Eros is always the hidden (or not so hidden) root cause for the collapse of ethics.

This is true both personally and collectively. We live in a moment of a worldwide and personal collapse of Eros. Our lack of Eros is poised to destroy

---

[4] We define Eros through what we refer to as the Eros equation (one of a series of what we call interior science equations):

Eros = Radical Aliveness x Desiring (Growing + Seeking) x Deeper Contact x Greater Wholeness x Self Actualization/Self Transcendence (Creation [Destruction])

There are good reasons for the formal language of the interior science equations in these writings, and the reader is invited to explore them on their own, in particular, in our work, David J. Temple, *First Principles and First Values: Forty-Two Propositions on CosmoErotic Humanism, the Meta-Crisis, and the World to Come* (World Philosophy and Religion, 2024).

the world. Humanity is currently experiencing what has come to be known as existential risk, a risk to our very existence, or what I will refer to as the Second Shock of Existence.

EXISTENTIAL RISK: THE SECOND SHOCK OF EXISTENCE

The first shock of existence is the death of the human being—the realization that we will die, which dawns in human consciousness at the beginning of history. We are not talking about the biological fact of death but the *existential* realization of death. Although the interior sciences disclose that death is a portal between two days (there is vast empirical,[5] philosophical,[6] and anthro-ontological evidence[7] for the continuity of consciousness[8]), death is also, in our own direct surface experience, a stark end. And that is obviously not a bug, but a feature in the system.

---

5 We refer to evidence gathered by the most serious of researchers, beginning with Henry and Edith Sedgwick at Cambridge University and William James at Harvard University, and continuing in highly rigorous form for the last 150 years, as recapitulated by Whiteheadian scholar David Ray Griffin in multiple volumes. See also, for example, Dean Radin, *Real Magic: Unlocking Your Natural Psychic Abilities to Create Everyday Miracles* (Potter/TenSpeed/Harmony, 2018), *The Conscious Universe: The Scientific Truth of Psychic Phenomena* (HarperCollins, 2010), and other books. Or see the earlier classic by Frederic William Henry Myers, *Human Personality and Its Survival of Bodily Death* (Longmans, Green, 1907).

6 This requires a cogent analysis of materialism and dualism, and the introduction of the far more cogent third possibility, which we have called "pan-interiority."

7 We discuss Anthro-Ontology in some depth in *First Principles and First Values*, and see also the fuller conversation in David J. Temple, *First Principles and First Values: Towards an Evolving Perennialism: Introducing the Anthro-Ontological Method*—both published by World Philosophy and Religion Press, in conjunction with Integral Publishers. For now, we will simply define it as an "innate and clear interior gnosis directly available to the human being."

8 See Dr. Marc Gafni and Dr. Zachary Stein's essay in preparation, "Beyond Death: Anthro-Ontology, Philosophy, and Empiricism." This essay is slated to appear in the book *Towards a World Religion: Homo Amor Essays*. The essay is also the ground for a larger book by the same authors, *Twelve Portals to Life Beyond Death: Responding to the Second Shock of Existence*, in which we discuss three forms of material: the empirical, the philosophical, and the anthro-ontological, and show how each form discredits the notion of death as the end.

Our first-person experience is that death ends this life. It is not the *totality* of our experience if we go deeper inside, but it is obviously intended to be the central, potent, and painful dimension of every human life. Indeed, as Ernest Becker potently reminded us, the denial of death is at our peril.

All the stories and all the plotlines and all the threads of living end at that moment. Whatever happens beyond, we have an actual experience of ending. **Paradoxically, that ending, the experience of the finality of mortality, is what presses us into life.** From the implicit demand of the first shock of existence, human beings were activated and pressed into creative emergence, and what emerged was all of human culture, both interior and exterior.

The second shock of existence is the realization of the potential death of all humanity. After all the stages of human history—matter, life, and mind in all of their stages of evolutionary unfolding—we have come to this place in the evolution of humanity, in which the gap between our exponentially expanding exterior technologies and our stalled (or even regressing) interior technologies of value has created dire catastrophic and existential risks.

This gap generates extraction models and exponential growth curves, rivalrous conflicts based on win/lose metrics, tragedies of the commons, and multipolar traps, in which everyone has to keep producing to the *n*th degree, including weaponized exponential threats to our very existence because we are afraid that the other parties are going to do it and not be transparent—hide it from us and then dominate us.

GENERATOR FUNCTIONS FOR EXISTENTIAL RISK

Let's outline clearly the main *generator functions for existential risk*.

Rivalrous conflicts governed by zero-sum, win/lose metrics. Rivalrous conflicts generate extraction models at the core of the economic system and exponential growth curves. Both of these drive and are driven by a contrived system of artificially manufactured desires and needs, delivered into culture by ever more precise forms of micro-targeting to individuals and groups through the ever more immersive environment of the internet.

Next, rivalrous conflicts and exponential growth curves animated by win/lose metrics generate **complicated, fragile world systems** highly vulnerable to myriad forms of collapse. Fragile local systems are made exponentially more fragile on a global level by our inability to meet global challenges with social, legal, political, economic, and ethical infrastructures that remain largely local.

All of this is a direct result of the failure to develop more adequate interior technologies that would be sufficiently compelling to displace "rivalrous conflict governed by win/lose metrics" as the motivational architecture for the human life world.

This failure has led to the conditions that will cause the implosion of systems that are already and quite literally on the brink of collapsing themselves. That's what we mean by the *second shock of existence*.

To recapitulate: the second shock of existence is not the death of the human being, but the potential death of humanity.

It is the *Death Star* moment of our species.

THE DECONSTRUCTION OF INTRINSIC VALUE

We stand in this moment poised between utopia and dystopia, at a time between worlds and a time between stories. We need a new Story of Value, eternal yet evolving, rooted in First Principles and First Values, which would become a universal grammar of value and a context for our diversity.

This is exactly what the Renaissance was. It was a time between worlds and a time between stories. In the Renaissance, we had recently been challenged by the Black Death, a pandemic that swept across Europe. The Black Death destroyed between a third to half of Europe and a huge part of

Asia. People died horrifically, brutally, in the streets. They had no idea how to meet this challenge, and so, in response to the Black Death, da Vinci and Ficino and their cohorts understood that they had to tell a new Story of Value.

That story was the story of modernity. Did they get it right?

- They got part of it right, which birthed, to use Jürgen Habermas' phrase, "the dignities of modernity," such as new ways of gathering information and universal human rights.
- But they also deconstructed the source of Value. They lost the basis for the Good, the True, and the Beautiful.

The basis used to be divine revelation: *God told us*. But this claim was owned by religion, and every religion began to overreach and over-claim. The revelation was thus often mediated through cultural categories and wasn't fully accurate.

> *Modernity threw out revelation, but was unable to establish a new basis for value.*

Value was just assumed to be real. As it says in the founding document of the American Revolution: *We hold these truths to be self-evident*—that is, *we don't really have a basis for value; we just take it as a given.*

In other words, modernity took out a loan of social capital from the traditional world. The source of value was never worked out.

And then, gradually, value began to collapse.

- The Universe Story began to collapse.
- The belief that the Good, the True, and the Beautiful are real began to collapse.
- The belief that Love is real began to collapse.

As Bertrand Russell is reported to have said, "I cannot see how to refute the arguments for the subjectivity of ethical values, but I find myself incapable of believing that all that is wrong with wanton cruelty is that I do not like it."

What do you do if you grew up in a world in which value is not real? A world without a source of value, without a Universe Story, without a story of human identity, without a story of desire, without a narrative of power?

In the words of W.B. Yeats, *the center does not hold.*

- You have a collapse at the very center of society, because you no longer have Eros.
- You no longer have a Reality in which value is real, and so you have this lingering sense of emptiness.
- You have a complete collapse at the very center.
- We become *the hollow men and the stuffed men*, gesture without form.

And that's the source of our current existential risk.

THE DEEPER ROOT CAUSE OF THE META-CRISIS: A GLOBAL INTIMACY DISORDER

Above, I have outlined the major generator functions of existential risk. But there is a deeper cause for the existential risk that lurks underneath the rivalrous conflict governed by win/lose metrics and the fragile systems they engender.

And we cannot take the Death Star down without discerning and addressing this. We have already alluded to this root cause above, but at this point we need to make it more explicit so that, from this context, the adequate root response will become clear.

Modernity threw out the revelation, but was unable to establish a new basis for value.

This ostensibly surprising statement can be understood in a few simple steps:

1. All of the catastrophic and existential risk challenges we face are global: from climate change to artificial intelligence, pandemics, systems collapse, and exponential arms races.
2. Every global challenge self-evidently requires a global solution.
3. Global solutions can only be implemented with global co-ordination.
4. Global co-ordination is impossible without global coherence.
5. Global coherence is only possible if there is a global resonance between the parts.
6. Global resonance is only possible if we have global intimacy.

ONLY A SHARED STORY OF VALUE CAN GENERATE GLOBAL INTIMACY

Global intimacy—just like intimacy in a couple—is only possible when there is a shared story.

Not just a shared history, but a shared Story of Value.

- It is only a shared global story that can generate a new emergent quality of intimacy: global intimacy.
- A shared Story of Value must be rooted in shared ordinating values, or what we have called evolving First Values and First Principles.
- Intimacy requires a shared grammar of value as a matrix for a shared Story of Value.

The global intimacy disorder is the root cause for existential risk. The global intimacy disorder underlies the core generator functions for existential risk.

The global intimacy disorder is rooted in the failure to experience ourselves in a field of shared intrinsic value. This failure derives from the deconstruction of value.

Indeed, it is wholly accurate to say that **the root cause of the two generator functions of existential risk is the failed story of intrinsic value, or what we might also call the breakdown of Eros.**

1. The first generator function is **the success story**. Our modern success story is rivalrous conflict governed by win/lose metrics, which violates all the terms of the Intimacy Equation: there is no shared identity and no mutuality of recognition, feeling, value or purpose, and instead of *relative* otherness, there is *alienated* otherness. Such a story generates complicated fragile systems with no allurement or intimacy between the parts, systems which optimize for efficiency (as an expression of win/lose metrics) and not for resiliency and life.
2. The second generator function is **the deconstruction of intrinsic value** itself. The deconstruction of value is the sense that human value does not participate in the intrinsic value of the Real, for the Real is dogmatically declared to have no intrinsic value. Thus, there is no shared identity between the interior of the human being and Reality. There is no common participation in a field of shared intrinsic value. Instead of being intimate with value, we are alienated from value. And only intrinsic value can arouse will: political, moral, and social will.

To sum up, without a shared grammar of value there is no global intimacy, and therefore no global coherence, and no global coordination in response to catastrophic and existential risk, which means, put simply, there will be, quite literally, no future.

HEALING THE GLOBAL INTIMACY DISORDER REQUIRES THE EVOLUTION OF INTIMACY

But we are not hopeless. On the contrary, we are filled with great hope. Hope is a memory of the future. That memory of the future *is* the direct hit that takes down the Death Star, the culture of death. **The direct hit must be**—as it has always been in history—**the emergence of a new stage of evolution.**

Crisis is an evolutionary driver, and every crisis is, at its core, a crisis of intimacy: from the oxygen crisis of the single cells dying which generated multicellular life at the dawn of existence, to the existential risk in this very moment.[9]

The direct hit is therefore structurally self-evident: the evolution of intimacy itself.

What is intimacy, as a structure of Cosmos all the way down and all the way up the evolutionary chain? We engage this inquiry in depth in other writings, but for now we will simply adduce what we have called the "Intimacy Equation":

> *Intimacy = shared identity in the context of [relative] otherness x mutuality of recognition x mutuality of pathos x mutuality of value x mutuality of purpose*

Intimacy is about the capacity of parts to generate a *shared identity* while retaining their otherness, or distinct identity. This requires multiple mutualities, including recognition, pathos (or feeling), value, and purpose. The parts must recognize and feel each other, even as they share value and purpose. But all of this must lead to intimate union—and not pathological

---

9   We demonstrate this principle in some depth in the multi-volume series, *The Universe: A Love Story* (forthcoming) (https://worldphilosophyandreligion.org/early-ontologies), *The Intimate Universe: Global Intimacy Disorder as Cause for Global Action Paralysis* (forthcoming), and in other writings of CosmoErotic Humanism.

fusion, where the distinct identity of the parts disappears—like subatomic particles that successfully become an atom, or two people who successfully become a couple.

THE DECONSTRUCTION OF VALUE IS THE DECONSTRUCTION OF INTIMACY

We have identified the global intimacy disorder as the root cause of existential risk. But the underlying ultimate failure of intimacy is the deconstruction of value itself.

The deconstruction of value means that human value does not participate in any sense of intrinsic value of the Real. This is not about individual *values*, but about *the Field of Value* that underlies all of them. **When the human being**—moved, often sincerely or even nobly, by myriad cultural, historical, and psychological confusions—**claims to have stepped out of the Field of Value, then intimacy itself is deconstructed.**

The deconstruction of value is the deconstruction of intimacy.

In the absence of a shared Story of Value, a story that is an authentic expression of Reality's Eros, a story rooted in *pseudo-Eros* takes center stage and becomes the generator function for existential risk. Our modern pseudo-Eros story is *rivalrous conflict governed by win/lose metrics*. Such a story catalyzes in its wake the second generator function of existential risk: *complicated fragile systems with no allurement or intimacy between the parts*. It is in that sense that we have argued that the first generator function for existential risk is the success story.

- The failure of intimacy is precisely the impotent experience that there is no shared identity between the interior of the human being and Reality. **There is no shared identity in the sense of any kind of common participation in a field of shared intrinsic value.**
- **But only a shared Story of Value can arouse the global will**

required to engage catastrophic and existential risk. For it is only global political, moral, and social will—and we can even say *erotic* will—that can generate the most Good, True and Beautiful world that we have always known is possible.

THE EVOLUTION OF LOVE IS THE TELLING OF A NEW STORY

Coupled with the Intimacy Equation is the scientifically grounded realization, in both the exterior and interior sciences, that Reality is a progressive deepening of intimacies, or, said slightly differently:

Reality is Evolution. Evolution is the evolution of intimacy.

- The evolution of intimacy requires—both personally and collectively—a deeper, more accurate discernment of the nature of our universe, ourselves, and our beloveds.
- This new discernment generates a new global Story of Value.
- The new global Story of Value generates an emergent, heretofore unseen global intimacy and heals the global intimacy disorder.

The new Story of Value is the direct hit that takes down the Death Star and replaces it with the hope that invokes the memory of our best future.

Global intimacy facilitates global coherence, which facilitates global coordination, which activates the possibility of our creative and effectively coordinated global responses to the global meta-crisis in its entirety and its specific expressions.

To solve Bertrand Russell's challenge—the apparent argument for the subjectivity of ethical values—**we have to reground value theory in eternal yet evolving First Principles and First Values, and articulate a new Story of Value.**

This is what we call CosmoErotic Humanism.

CosmoErotic Humanism—together with other emergent strands—**needs to become the ground of a world religion as a context for our diversity**. We need religion, even as we need science, to articulate a shared global grammar of value.

As we said at the beginning, our choice is simple: love or die.

- To love means to participate in the evolution of love, which is the evolution of the human Story of Value.
- To love means to evolve and activate a new cultural enlightenment—rooted in a new narrative of identity, a new narrative of value, a new narrative of intimate communion, a new narrative of desire, a new narrative of power—all of which will birth new narratives of economics and politics.
- The evolution of love is the telling of a new Story.

The new Story that must be told is a love story, for in fact that is the deepest truth of Reality, rooted in the best exterior and interior sciences, that we have at this moment in time:

- Reality is not merely a fact. Reality is a story.
- Reality is not an ordinary story. Reality is a love story.
- Reality is not an ordinary love story. Reality is an Outrageous Love Story.

Story doesn't mean it's *made-up*.

It means doing the hard work of integrating the validated insights of the traditional world, the modern world, and the postmodern world.

This is the intention at the heart of telling the new Story of CosmoErotic Humanism.

ABOUT THIS VOLUME

We live in a moment of global action paralysis. In the gap between our ability to feel the pain of the world and our ability to heal the pain of the world, we close our hearts. We close our hearts because we are paralyzed.

This book explores the global action paralysis caused by people all over the world being afraid to join the symphony. The global action paralysis is rooted in a global intimacy disorder. Only by healing the global intimacy disorder will we be able to heal the global action paralysis. We can heal the global intimacy disorder only by restoring the fabric of intimacy that is at the core of Reality.

It's not that we have lost intimacy on a global level; we have never had it. We never evolved to global intimacy. We have exiled intimacy to only human or romantic relationships. We have exiled intimacy to sexuality.

The exile of intimacy has left us disconnected, even dissociated—not just from each other, but from the evolutionary process itself. For intimacy is the very fabric of Reality itself. We live in an Intimate Universe.

Evolution is the evolution of intimacy. Reality is not a fact, it is a story; it is going somewhere. It has telos, direction. The story of evolution is not an accidental chance story. It is not random. It is driven by Evolutionary Eros. Evolution is the love story of the Universe.

This book is an invitation to reclaim intimacy as the core structure of Reality. We live in an Intimate Universe. To heal the intimacy disorder at the core of our global crisis, we must evolve intimacy and step into a

ABOUT THIS VOLUME

Planetary Awakening in Love through Unique Self Symphonies. We need a new politics of love, a politics beyond polarization, where the future is co-created in social synergy.

We are not just passive observers. We are able to say *Yes* to the next chapter in the unfolding story of evolution. We are not just witnessing history; we are participating in the evolution of love.

This is the transition from "I have a dream" to "We have a dream." We are awakening into what Marc and Barbara have called "The Wheel of Co-Creation 2.0," where we no longer compete for limited resources but collaborate to create the more beautiful world we know is possible. We do not compete. We join genius. We co-create. We move from win/lose metrics into synergistic democracy. We move from a politics of separation into a politics of evolutionary love.

When we gather in circles of co-creation—what Barbara Marx Hubbard called Syncons for synergistic convergence—we create something new. We enter into what we in CosmoErotic Humanism[1] calls a Unique Self Symphony, where each Unique Self[2] plays its unique instrument in the symphony, contributing their unique gift to the larger whole.

We come together in social synergy to bring together our unique genius into the Wheel of Co-Creation, which is the foundation of synergistic democracy. It does not ask, "Who is right?" but rather: "What do we need to create together that we cannot create alone?"

We are activating the Wheel of Co-Creation, carrying us through to the next stage in the evolution of democracy, beyond crisis, beyond Armageddon, and into a Planetary Awakening in Love through Unique Self Symphonies.

You have an utterly unique role to play. Your action is needed by humanity. Your action is desired by all of Reality. The direction of all of Reality is

---

[1] For a deep dive into CosmoErotic Humanism, see David J. Temple, *First Principles and First Values: Forty-Two Propositions on CosmoErotic Humanism* (2024).
[2] See Marc Gafni, *Your Unique Self: The Radical Path to Personal Enlightenment* (2012).

toward the evolution of love, and that evolution is occurring in you, as you, and through you, right now.

These pages offer you a new and profound way of knowing your place in the Universe. They offer you a path to awaken your Unique Self—an irreducible unique configuration of love and intimacy that never was, is, or will be ever again—and as such you have a unique gift to give that only you can give.

Join with others in Unique Self Symphony to become an agent of intimacy in your unique corner of the world. The only response to the outrageous pain of the world is Outrageous Love. Or said differently, only a new politics of evolutionary love can heal the global intimacy disorder.

Volume 2

These oral essays are edited talks delivered by Marc Gafni and Barbara Marx Hubbard between January and March 2017.

CHAPTER ONE

CELEBRATING EPIPHANY: THE BIRTH OF THE NEW HUMAN AND THE NEW HUMANITY

Episode 11 — January 7, 2017

EPIPHANY OF HOMO UNIVERSALIS, A NEW HUMAN

The Epiphany is an ancient Christian feast to celebrate the birth of the baby Jesus and the visit by the Three Wise Men, who somehow realized that, in this baby, **God was showing up as something radically new.**

What actually happened there in that first Epiphany? How do we celebrate Epiphany?

Another meaning of epiphany is *manifestation*. Something radically new manifested, and people were able to recognize it. This baby turns out to be able to create in abundance, to transform the world, to fill it with love, to die and be reborn in a new body, and to tell us that we would be doing the works that He did and greater works than these would we do in the fullness of time.

That is what happened at that Epiphany. And before the crucifixion, Jesus told us this very amazing phrase: *take, eat, this is my body*.

"Take, drink, this is my blood given to you to transform into new beings."

The miracle of our epiphany is that it is all coming true when we view the story and promise of Jesus that we will do the works that He did, and greater works than these will we do in the fullness of time. If we look at our current life with evolutionary eyes, we see that it is all coming true.

Let us commit to infuse love into the new powers of humanity, which means that we are going to become new humans.

In celebrating the birth of the baby Jesus, let us celebrate the birth of baby *Homo universalis*. Let us celebrate the birth of:

- ourselves becoming new,
- becoming Unique Selves,
- joining in a Unique Self Symphony coordinated by the self-organizing universe,
- awakening the whole world to our potential to evolve into co-creative humans.

We can produce in abundance. We may travel with the speed of light. We may evolve new bodies. We can build new worlds. The manifestation of the baby Jesus is now declared to be the manifestation of the baby *Homo universalis*, the new human.

We are literally announcing a *manifestation*, for the very first time, in relationship to the Epiphany of Jesus' manifestation. **Affirm the reality that we are, each of us, a manifestation of the whole process of creation, of the 13.8 billion years, in every atom, molecule, cell, and brain.**

We are coming alive, conscious of ourselves as co-creators, gaining the powers that Jesus and many other great avatars from all great religions actually had—and far more—able to heal, transform, and prolong life. We are singing praises of the manifestation of the new human: to cultivate it, to care for it, to love it, to give birth and send this new human forth into the *politics of love,* to rebuild Earth and carry out this mystical tradition in real time, to affirm that we are good, that we are whole, to affirm the new powers that the new human has been given—spiritual, social, and technological.

Whatever background we come from, we can be born as new humans.

WE ARE SPIRITUALLY INCORRECT EVANGELICALS

You cannot wing holiness. What we are doing is wildly ecstatic; it is deep in the heart, and it is *precise.* We want to be precise, and ritual is precise. We are trying to weave a new evolutionary, mystical magic, to convene in community.

We are in Bethlehem.

We are in Mecca.

We are in Jerusalem.

We are founding something new, and it requires us to bring all of us.

Ein kedusha be'li ha'chana, my teacher used to say, **There's no holiness without preparation.**

You cannot wing it—you cannot wing holiness.

You've got to bring all of yourself.

We are thinking about:

- What is the right holy word?
- How do we come together in full presence?

- How do we come together and storm heaven?
- How do we storm heaven, which is right here on Earth, and reveal together that the next Buddha is a sangha in this Unique Self Symphony, the new possibility of possibility?

Let's make a connection between *resonance* and *prayer*.

Whenever someone is talking and we are listening deeply, we are feeling each other. Feel each other in space, in the holiest way.

It's so important to *feel* into and be *fully present*. Fully present, nothing left out. That's how we feel. No distance, nothing left out, no one is someplace else. That's resonance.

You cannot fool God! You cannot put on a show. Either we are all here, fully present, alive, awake, giving everything, or we are not here at all. That's what an epiphany is.

EPIPHANY IS TRANSCENDING THE REGULAR

Epiphany means, **how do we get *out* of the regular?**

Can we get out of the regular? We can be doing the same thing, and it just becomes regular.

But actually, *Regular* is *regel*, meaning pilgrimage. When you go on a pilgrimage, it is what is called in the Bible, going up by foot (*aliya le regel*). Going up by foot means *transcending the regular*. That's what an epiphany is: *to transcend the regular;* that's pilgrimage.

Can we get out of the regular?

- Are we willing to surprise ourselves?
- Are we willing to be surprised?
- Are we willing to transcend the regular?

We are going to climb this mountain *together*.

God is the possibility of possibility. That's *not* regular, that means that something new is born that never existed before.

We are not here to do life again like we did last week! Heck, that's the whole point. Let's make it **new** every week. Can we show up as new every week? Can we let go of the regular?

THERE IS NO COMPELLING VISION OF POSTMODERNITY

Postmodernity, the liberal world, said *you only get to be a hero if you are a victim*. All heroic books are about victims. The great news is:

- Every victim we want to *hear*.
- Every victim we want to *honor*.
- Every victim we want to *embrace*.
- Every victim we want to *transform*.

The bad news is—there are too many people claiming victimhood and **not enough people claiming their power**.

There is no positive vision.

- What's the liberal vision of **duty**?
- What's the liberal vision of **honor**?
- What's the liberal vision of **integrity**?

What's the liberal vision of **an ethic, a shared global ethic for a global civilization?**

For the first time in history, love in postmodernity didn't quite evolve.

Do you get that? It's a big deal!

Premodernity had a big vision, the traditional religions. Lots of mistakes—a little xenophobic, a little homophobic; they were all trying to kill each other. But actually, Christ had some insight. Buddha had some insight; Lao

Tzu had some insight. Confucius had something going on there, the Jews, too. All of it was not bad, but all had weaknesses.

Modernity came and critiqued the values of premodernity. Modernity added the good stuff and did a great job.

But then **postmodernity** critiqued modernity because modernity was lost in its own narratives; too many people were excluded. Too many people were not part of the story. Postmodernity critiqued modernity and its vision of love, its vision of duty, ethics, and honor.

> *What did postmodernity forget to do? It forgot to offer a new vision, a new Universe Story.*

So, what did the president of the United States, Donald Trump, do? He realized—not consciously, none of this is conscious—there is no compelling vision of postmodernity in the liberal world.

When evolution doesn't move forward, it stalls, and then it meanders, as our friend Michael Murphy likes to say. Evolution can even move backward.

Trump reanimated the shadows of capitalism, the shadows of business. In truth, though, we're not going to correct this until we actually get straight that we've got to *offer a new vision*.

We bring a new vision. We are bringing the good news! We've got to go into *dharma*, into prayer, into God, and we've got to participate together.

We are evangelicals!

What does that mean?

Not that we're fundamentalists, but that **we are bringing the good news, we are telling a new Universe Story.**

CELEBRATING EPIPHANY

CAN WE OPEN UP TO EPIPHANY?

Steve Jobs wasn't embarrassed to bring the good news; he called Apple people evangelicals. In the entire Apple world, they are evangelical. Wow!

We are liberals, but we either don't have the good news or are too embarrassed to bring the good news; we just have social constructions of Reality.

Really? Everything—ethics, loyalty, goodness—is all social constructions of Reality?

No!

If we say *that* then the fundamentalists are going to hijack God, hijack ethics, and hijack the whole story.

My good friends, we are evangelicals. We are not politically correct; we are *spiritually incorrect*. We are bringing the good news.

The good news is not about any particular person's charisma, it's about the charisma of the good news. Charisma means Spirit falling through, the vision of evolution in which we are *aligned* with the evolutionary impulse, awakening as the personal face of evolution.

We know that Reality has a personal face: Reality is not just the Infinity of Power, it's the Infinity of Intimacy.

The Infinity of Intimacy, wow! That is an epiphany. Do you get it?

When you realize that Reality is not just the Infinity of Power, that Reality is the Infinity of Intimacy—when that goes *in*, that's an epiphany. Epiphany means, *We get it. It's not regular. We are willing to get something new.*

Much of the internet is built on confirmation bias: confirm what you already know; refuse to learn anything new. The internet can be an echo chamber. The news feeds on the internet confirm what you already believe; you are never challenged.

The internet is built in a way that is not open-sourced and decentralized, with everybody talking to everybody. That was the vision, to open up to new epiphanies. But the internet has become a place of closed environments or echo chambers, where confirmation biases are confirmed time and time again rather than challenged.

So, can we open up to epiphanies? Let us wake up *into* this. We've got to offer this new vision.

EVOLVING PRAYER: GOD, LOVE ME OPEN!

Part of our new vision is that we are going to evolve prayer.

What does prayer mean? Prayer means not just God having our experience; prayer means that God *holds* us.

Do you get that, that *God holds us*?

The god you don't believe in doesn't exist. It's not the primitive God. It's God which is the personal force of evolution that's not just third-person evolutionary impulse, but the *Infinity of Intimacy*.

If we love each other, that love that we feel personally for each other isn't limited to us. It comes from the personal face of all of Reality, the Infinity of Intimacy which is the Infinite Power of Cosmos,

- all of the light years,
- all of the complexity of physics,
- all of the complexity of chemistry,
- all of the exponential power of nuclear power which is *but a pale reflection* (borrowing the phrase from *Hamlet*).

All of the infinite power of Cosmos is sitting in a chair looking at you saying, *Oh my god, I love you so much.*

You feel the intensity of the divine gaze—and in that gaze you become whole. You know that God *sees* you, *loves* you, *yearns* for you, *lusts* for you.

That's what the original texts say: *HaKadosh Baruch Hu mit'aveh la'asot dira ba-tachtonim,* or God desires to live in the incarnate place of humanness; God desires you.

God desires you in every second which is why the celibate nuns and priests can talk about being penetrated open by Jesus.

When you realize that God knows us, desires us, adores us, loves us, and holds us, that the Infinite Intelligence of all of Reality yearns for us:

- to turn to Her,
- to turn to Him,
- to offer our prayer
- and affirm the dignity of personal need,
- and ask for everything,

…then we can ask for everything, for everyone because we break our egocentricity. And we ask, and our ask gets wider, but it doesn't come from an automatic mind, it comes from our heart.

Our heart. *Rachmana Leba Baei,* the words say in Aramaic.

God wants the heart. God wants full presence. God wants us to feel each other's pain and joy. God feels our pain and our joy in every second.

Sometimes men may live lives of quiet desperation. Thoreau was right in *Walden*. But men and women *never* live lives of lonely desperation because, in every moment of desperation, God is holding us. **God is the Infinity of Intimacy that knows our name and holds us even when we don't know *She*'s there.** The god you don't believe in doesn't exist.

- We are willing to be new.
- We are willing to prepare.
- We are willing to show up and give everything.

- We are willing to storm heaven and bring it to Earth as if it's the only thing that matters.

It is the only thing that matters.

We pray for each other. We pray for ourselves because **prayer affirms the dignity of personal need.**

We ask for everything because the gates are open, all the gates are open.

We offer our prayer up, and we pray for everyone who can't pray, we pray for everyone.

We pray to the Infinity of Intimacy.

Al-Farabi[1] said that the prophet uses imagination. Imagination is the source that opens the deepest truth. We imagine what's real, and we know that God is listening to us in every moment. And God is sitting in front of us knowing our name. The Infinity of Intimacy—all of the laws of physics in its intimate, personal face.

> *We know that our prayer moves God, moves All-That-Is.*

Offer up prayer! Have the audacity to step in. God wants the heart. Dare to pray. Prayer affirms the dignity of personal need. To be like God, to be like Christ, to be like Buddha is, *I feel you.*

Find your most intimate words, your most true words.

God—the Infinity of Intimacy—is in front of us! And we begin to actually pray for each other. We feel each other's need. We feel each other.

We can be speaking all the spiritual words in the world and be lost in egocentricity. Or we can soften our hearts, unguard our hearts, let our

---

[1] Al-Farabi, renowned early Islamic philosopher.

hearts break open, and take each other in. That's the beginning of a politics of evolutionary love, the beginning of intimacy, the beginning of epiphany.

TIPPING THE SCALES OF EVOLUTION TOWARDS MORE LIFE AND MORE LOVE

We are celebrating the epiphany of the amazing revelation of the story of creation that has only recently come to the human species. We used to think it was done by an outside force or by accident, but we are discovering that **the story of creation has a true line from the original Big Bang.**

Imagine the original Big Bang and feel your origin in that moment when the entire pattern of the Universe was established.

Out of that, go through the billions and billions of years—every turn of the spiral. Go into the core of that spiral. See it as the impulse of the divine, creative intelligence, supra-mental genius of creation, coming from Source, coming from the Field of Consciousness creating single cells, multicells, animals, and humans.

Bring in all the great humans that came before us. Particularly, on Epiphany-day, let's bring Jesus into the story of evolution. Let's see the birth of that little baby, whom people recognized was holding something new, something great.

What was he holding? The precognitive reality of what we are becoming: "You will do the works that I do, and greater works than these will you do in the fullness of time because I went to the Father."

What did He mean by that? The Father, I call the *source of creation*.

When we go to the Father, the Mother, the Source, the creative impulse of evolution, what we are going into is the **passionate potential of evolution itself in every one of us.**

Take baby Jesus as a first symbol in our culture of the new human. Take that big sweep from the life of Jesus to all the efforts of Western civilization and now global civilization, to gain the powers of Gods, the powers of the young Jesus. We have achieved that.

We are right at the threshold of either destroying ourselves with the powers we've been given, or evolving ourselves through conscious evolution, conscious, ethical, loving evolution in the direction of the billions of years toward higher consciousness, freedom, and order.

What we are doing is gathering to ourselves the awesome Reality of the story that has created us.

We are able to say *Yes* to the next chapter in the unfolding story of evolution.

All of us, for the first time in the history of humanity, have one sacred story, for all of us, all of us! That's the story of evolution.

The beauty of saying *Yes* to the story of evolution in ourselves—our Epiphany-day—is that we can see ahead, toward a vision of what our species can become if we, who know this, hold it together and reach out as far as we can to humanity everywhere at the very moment of devolution or evolution. Then **what we are literally doing is tipping the scales of evolution toward more life, more love, more freedom, more consciousness, and more awareness.**

- We are bringing our noosphere, our thinking layer of Earth, our planetary nervous system into the awareness of the emergence of everything that we can do that's good.
- We are aiming at the awakening of our nervous system on a planetary scale to that which we are universally and individually incarnating *en masse*.

All the people who are saying *Yes* to evolution now are gathering their force.

We have a vision of a Planetary Awakening in love through Unique Self Symphonies.

Now, what is the Unique Self Symphony?

The Unique Self Symphony draws together Unique Selves—irreducible unique expressions of the LoveIntelligence and LoveBeauty that is the initiating and animating energy of All-That-Is. And we create not a top-down but a bottom-up self-organizing Universe in which we are all giving our unique gift, and we unleash entrepreneurial gorgeousness that changes and transforms the world like nothing else can.

Our nervous system is coming alive in a continual epiphany because the way evolution works is by self-organizing.

We are primary agents of evolution who have said *Yes* to giving our gift to the world and to one another toward a planetary awakening, which is going to create a vision of a universal humanity born into a universe of trillions of planets and galaxies.

We are celebrating the miracles, the miraculous story of the entire process of creation as *a love story*.

WHY IS THE UNIVERSE A LOVE STORY?

For the first time, we realize that the essential nature of Reality is:

- Not a fact; **it's a story**, step one.
- Step two, it's not an ordinary story; **it's a love story**.
- Step three, when we say *a love story*, we don't mean a kind of New Age aphorism; we don't mean a Harlequin romance. It's not an ordinary story; **it's an Outrageous Love Story.** Outrageous Love is Evolutionary Love.
- Evolutionary Love is not mere human sentiment. **It's the heart of existence itself.** It's the love that *allures* Reality all the way up and all the way down. Because Reality is desire,

- allurement, and love, all the way up and all the way down until it appears in us, as us, and through us. Evolution, the allurement of love, becomes conscious.
- Step five, we realize that not only is The Universe: A Love Story, but that *our* love story is not by accident. **Our life is a love story that is inextricably bound up with and needed by All-That-Is.** Our love story is part of *the Universe: a Love Story*.
- The Universe: a Love Story cannot be successful or realize itself *unless* we give the unique gift, the unique presence, and the unique quality of intimacy that comes out of *our* love story.

This is why our sutra is not ordinary love—a strategy of the ego—but *Outrageous Love*. The sutra is: **We live in a world of outrageous pain. The only response to outrageous pain is Outrageous Love.**

We declare that **the noosphere—the universal intelligence system—is aware of us.** The universe is responsive to requests. The universe is listening, and we are coding our planetary nervous system with these memes. This is not a fiction of our imagination; this is the way evolution works.

The words we declare are becoming Reality in the love we infuse our words with, together. We are actually bringing forth this birth by our presence, now.

There was a guy named Feuerbach[2] who said, *God is a figment of your imagination*. But you know what? Let's tell Feuerbach, *Our imagination is a figment of God*.

---

2 Ludwig Feuerbach was a nineteenth-century German philosopher and anthropologist best known for his critique of religion and his argument that the concept of God is a projection of human qualities and desires. In his influential work, *The Essence of Christianity* (1841), Feuerbach proposed that God does not exist independently of human consciousness but is rather an idealized figment of the human imagination.

THE DIVINE WHISPER: SYNCHRONICITY

Feel into it. **We live in an Intimate Universe.** Can you feel that?

In an Intimate Universe there are epiphanies happening all over the place that whisper particularly *to us*.

In the Aramaic that Jesus spoke, we call it *Lechisha De'orayta*, which means *the divine whisper*.

Aramaic texts say if you are sitting in a restaurant, and as you are sitting in the restaurant, you've been thinking about, *Should I move to Jamaica or not?* You hear someone at the next table talking about, *Wow, there are these really great houses available in Jamaica!*

The Zohar and the Aramaic texts say that's a divine voice. It's *a divine whisper*.

Jung talked about *synchronicity*. What he meant was we live in an Intimate Universe that is speaking to each of us; it is *Lechisha*, whispering in our ear.

Libby Roderick sang it for us. [*See Appendix.*]

> "How Could Anyone" — Libby Roderick[3]
>
> *How could anyone ever tell you*
>   *you were anything less than beautiful?*
> *How could anyone ever tell you*
>   *you were less than whole?*
> *How could anyone fail to notice*
>   *that your loving is a miracle—*
>   *how deeply you're connected to my soul?*

---

[3] Libby Roderick, "How Could Anyone Ever Tell You," on *If You See a Dream* (Turtle Island Records, 1990).

The truth is in the aftertaste. We hold it so softly. We hold it audaciously. **The true humility is absolute audacity when we realize *She*'s speaking through us.** She wants to and needs to speak through us.

Let's conclude with a story. This is the epiphany. Are we willing to receive epiphany?

> It was on a holy day, a day which was the holiest of holy days. The master turned to his students, *Who shall live, and who shall die?*
>
> On that particular day, the disciples are quaking and trembling because…
>
> *Who knows where we are going to be next week?*
>
> *Who knows where we are going to be next year, next New Year?*
>
> *Who shall live, and who shall die?*
>
> *Who by the sword?*
>
> *Who by sickness?*
>
> *Who by delight—and who quietly and gently?*
>
> *Who shall prosper, and who shall fail?*
>
> We don't know. Everyone is praying for themselves, lost in the egocentric predicament.
>
> The master says to the students, *Do you want to know the holy secret?*
>
> They say, *Yes, yes!*
>
> The master says, *Do you want to know the holy secret that allows us to actually cheat the angel of death, that allows us to all live and all live together?*
>
> *Yes, yes.*
>
> *Are you really sure you want to know?*
>
> *Yes, tell us.*

> He says, *Here's the secret. Turn to the person next to you and say,* ***I'm not willing to be written in the Book of Life without you.***

Reach out to others and say, *I am not willing to be written in the Book of Life without you.*

When that happens, when you can feel others, and they can feel you, that's intimacy.

Feel me feeling you: we are born as co-creative humans now awakening the Universe to our presence.

CHAPTER TWO

PRINCIPLES OF A PERSONAL POLITICS OF EVOLUTIONARY LOVE

Episode 12 — January 14, 2017

A POLITICS OF EVOLUTIONARY LOVE

Who are you?

This is the first principle of a politics of Evolutionary Love: *You are an irreducibly Unique Self and a unique expression of Outrageous Love.*

As an irreducibly Unique Self, you are an irreducibly unique expression of the LoveIntelligence and LoveBeauty that is the initiating, animating energy of All-That-Is.

That is the answer to the question, *Who are you?*

You are God's unique intimacy. As such, you have a unique perspective and a unique gift to give that is needed by All-That-Is.

That is the first principle of being a citizen—**to be a citizen is the greatest privilege in the world**—to be a citizen is to be a Unique Self and a unique expression of Outrageous Love.

We open our hearts to all who have been left out. We are imbued with the passion of Evolutionary Love such that it fills absolutely every fiber of our beings as co-creators. We feel the impulse of Evolutionary Love coming from Source—coming from the original consciousness, carrying us through the billions of years—expressing through us directly in the passion of complete and total fulfillment of our creativity and as our gift to the world.

> *We experience ourselves as an evolutionary impulse, in person, alive— the impulse of Evolutionary Love.*

Why do we say the entire impulse of billions of years is Evolutionary Love and is alive in us?

One could ask, how could it be love with all the pain that has been felt way before we got here? Or, billions of species went extinct, the five mass extinctions? If I were a creator God attempting to create an expression of Evolutionary Love, it appears to me in all humility that this is a Universe of intrinsic freedom with an intrinsic purpose to evolve that allowed for it to be a discovery process, that allowed for all the creatures that came before us, each of which totally yearned to give forth their own potential.

It is the nature of life to do that. God put into every creature that came before us a yearning to realize their unique potential.

See the struggle that must have been—electrons, protons, neutrons, early multicellular organisms all the way up.

Feel that very same impulse that created the Universe, driving through us as our unique impulse, to give our full potential self into **a world that is at the threshold of crisis and devolution or birth and evolution.**

Experience the billions of years of evolution coming through as your Unique Self, Evolutionary Unique Self, meaning that our Unique Self is a direct experience of the billions of years of evolution in person.

Get in touch with the impulse of creation inside you, knowing that it has coded in it all the journey that it has been on, and it also has coded in it a memory of the future. **That memory of the future is the passionate desire of your Evolutionary Unique Self to fully express itself in love.**

This is what we mean by taking the lid off the top and praying without limitation because the God in us, as us, has chosen this generation of all the generations that ever came before us, to express that love without reservation.

- Take a moment to love every single person who has been left out.
- Take your passionate love of creativity and touch into the hearts of all our brothers and sisters and children worldwide who perceive they have been left out of the process of creation.
- Dedicate the purpose of all of humanity to have the opportunity to express to the fullest possible extent the beauty of their desire to create and the beauty of their desire to love.

We call on the Unique Self Symphony to realize that every voice, everywhere in the world, has a unique note of beauty, excellence, and creativity to give into a symphony which can result in a planetary awakening in love.

Open your arms. All of us who have been privileged to know that we are evolving humans, reach out to all the humans who are also evolving.

In our principles of evolutionary politics, there is the Unique Self expressed in Evolutionary Love, such that Evolutionary Unique Self joins with every other self who is yearning to give their potential, to create an Evolutionary Unique Self Symphony heard for the very first time in human history.

For the very first time, this level of evolutionary potential and realization of the intention of creation has been affirmed as the purpose of an Evolutionary Church. I invite evolutionary mosques and evolutionary temples to take up the one story of creation that we all have been given.

It is the new Universe Story.

We don't have ten narratives here. For the first time, we have one narrative. It is the Universe Story. As we enter the evolutionary aspect of that story, **we imbue it as our own potential to love. That is where Evolutionary Love comes in.**

- There is no doubt whatsoever that this is the purpose of evolution.
- There is no doubt whatsoever that this is the creative potential of every human being on Earth.

Let us bring it to the world, in all our diplomatic relationships and in all our relationships and associations with Russia, with Iran, with Egypt, with Pakistan. With every country. **The people everywhere joining us.**

FIVE CORE PRINCIPLES OF A POLITICS OF EVOLUTIONARY LOVE

What are our principles?

FIRST PRINCIPLE: YOU ARE A UNIQUE SELF

The first principle of a personal politics of Evolutionary Love is, *you are a Unique Self.*

Who are you?

You are a Unique Self.

SECOND PRINCIPLE: UNIQUENESS IMPLIES NEED

We are needed by all that is. Reality needs our service.

Reality manifests only what it needs.

If we tinker around, create something, and spend thousands and billions of years creating it, and zillions of synchronicities come together to manifest it, that means we need it.

- We need it aesthetically, for its beauty.
- We need it because of the way it can serve.
- We need it for what it can express in the world.

Each of us is irreducibly unique, with about 50 trillion cells, millions of miles of nerve cables. We are processes of dazzling complexity, which are utterly unique, unlike any others, in our immune system, our DNA, our cellular signature, our atomic signature.

If all that is true, it means we are needed. We are not extra. As a Unique Self, you are irreducible, irreplaceable, needed by All-That-Is.

The second principle of a personal politics of Evolutionary Love is: **You are needed by All-That-Is. Reality needs your service.**

THIRD PRINCIPLE: YOU HAVE A UNIQUE GIFT

Your unique gift is an expression of your irreducibly unique perspective and your unique quality of intimacy, your unique taste. Unique perspective comes together with our unique quality of intimacy.

We have an irreducibly unique perspective, even from a physical perspective, as we are always located at a particular place in the space-time continuum. That is in the exterior.

On the interior, we are a unique perspective of Reality. It is our *slant*, as it were, on reality. Our irreducibly unique perspective comes together with our unique taste.

What do we mean by unique taste? Pull up the image of a friend in your mind, that is your friend's taste. Pull up a different friend, that is them. We don't confuse the tastes of people.

That is the unique quality of intimacy that a person is. So, if we sit with a friend in silence—that silence will be different than if that friend sits with someone else in silence.

> *We are not just a unique perspective;*
> *we are a unique quality of intimacy.*

Our unique perspective comes together with our unique quality of intimacy.

Those are two principles of uniqueness:

- We are a unique perspective.
- We are a unique quality of intimacy.

Those two come together to form *your* unique gift. You have a unique gift to be given that comes from living into *your* unique intimacy, *your* seeing with *your* unique perspective, and *your* unique gift can be given only by you.

So, three principles of a politics of Evolutionary Love are:

- First: you are a Unique Self.
- Second: you are needed by All-That-Is. Uniqueness implies need. You are needed by All-That-Is.
- Third: What is needed is your unique gift, which is the emanation, the expression, the coming together of your unique quality of intimacy and your irreducibly unique perspective.

We need to enumerate them, so we can see the principles. That's why there are Four Noble Truths, and why there are Ten Commandments.

FOURTH PRINCIPLE: EVOLUTION IS LOVE IN ACTION

This is the principle of the evolutionary impulse. You are not just a Unique Self, you are a unique expression of the LoveIntelligence which is not ordinary love; it is Outrageous Love or Evolutionary Love. **Evolutionary Love is the love which sources All-That-Is and that drives all of Reality.**

Let us feel the fourth principle. Reality is not a fact; it is a story. That means, it is going somewhere. It is not an ordinary story. It is a love story. It is not an ordinary love story, but an Evolutionary Love Story.

Evolutionary Love drives the whole process. Evolution is the fourth principle: *love in action.*

The fourth principle comes together with the first principle—Unique Self—which means you are personally implicated in the story.

You are carrying the impulse of Evolutionary Love, uniquely needed.

We know that democracy does not just reside in politics, that **democracy resides in our presence and behavior of creating together a world equal to our potential.** We are not even limited to what has been called democracy with this degree of love. It is not about voting, it is about creating.

Everyone is needed! That brings us so beautifully to that planetary sense.

We need Donald Trump. We need Melania Trump. That is critical to understand. We need Donald Trump to be the most successful president ever in the history of the United States because *that* is bigger than politics.

Barack Obama is in his deepest center when the ego falls away, and he is in Barack Obama-ness. He is Reality having a Barack Obama experience. Barack Obama was so graceful in his farewell. He wished deeply for President Trump to be the best president that America could possibly have because that is good for America, which is good for the world—there is no split.

PRINCIPLES OF A PERSONAL POLITICS OF EVOLUTIONARY LOVE

Each person is a Unique Self, an irreducibly Unique Self, needed by All-That-Is.

FIFTH PRINCIPLE: WE ARE A UNIQUE SELF SYMPHONY

Out of our fifth principle everything comes together. We are at a moment where we need to move from mastermind, which is Unique Self, to metamind.

Metamind is Unique Self Symphony. Unique Self Symphony means—our ultimate commitment is to *We the People*. *We the People* are not just an aggregate of separate selves as Bentham, and Mill, and Hobbes thought.

In this new principle, this new politics of principle five, of a politics of Evolutionary Love, **we realize that we are a Unique Self Symphony and that the Universe is self-organizing.**

The Universe self-actualizes and self-organizes, just like an ant hill self-organizes; every ant knows what to do based on pheromone secretions. This is similar to slime molds, which kind of look like diarrhea on the floor of the forest. Slime molds are a multicellular blob that splits up into single cells, looks like it is completely dissipated, then comes together perfectly as a multicellular unit again. It is able to do all sorts of elegant and complex processes even though it has the most simple structure. Does science understand how that works? Who is the general that's running the slime mold?

And along came Alan Turing. (Remember the movie about Turing, who cracked the Nazi codes in World War II?) The early computers were called Turing machines. Turing wrote an essay at Bell Labs in 1947 called *Morphogenesis*. It is about the self-organizing universe, which means the universe self-actualizes.

We are going to add to Turing these interiors: the universe self-organizes toward:

- More consciousness
- More goodness
- More love
- More creativity

This is critical. It means self-organizing happens, not just at the level of slime molds or ant hills but also at the human level.

THE STRANGE ATTRACTOR *IS* UNIQUE SELF

How does the Universe self-organize to higher levels of love? What is the strange attractor?[4] What is the strange attractor for Unique Self Symphony? What is the strange attractor for a self-organizing Universe?

We are attracted to give our unique gift. We are allured to give our unique gift. When we *all* begin giving our unique gift—addressing the unique need in our unique circle of intimacy and influence—then we begin to have a bottom-up politics, not a top-down politics.

Ultimately, it is *our* turn.

> *We are the citizens. We are the people.*
> *We are the Unique Self Symphony.*

- It is our city.
- It is our streets.
- It is our neighborhoods.
- It is our institutions.
- It is our country.
- It is our town.

---

[4] A strange attractor is a concept in chaos theory that is used to describe the behavior of chaotic systems. A strange attractor... can predict certain characteristics of a chaotic pattern in great detail without being able to assign a specific spatial location to the pattern (Todd Podzemny, www.allthescience.org).

- It is our village.
- It is our laws.

The tragedy of this last 2016 election was that so few people voted. We have got to vote. We have got to get up and do it. It is our turn!

When we rise up as a self-organizing Universe, we rise up as a Unique Self Symphony—each of us giving our Unique Gifts; then we will have articulated the fifth principle.

Let us do this together. Let us articulate together a personal politics of Evolutionary Love.

MEDITATION: BREATHE FROM THE DEEP IMPULSE OF EVOLUTION WITHIN US

Breathe from the deep impulse of evolutionary creativity within each of us.

Breathe all the way from the mind of God up through that evolutionary impulse's extraordinary powers of creation—for billions and billions of years bringing more life, more consciousness, more freedom, more complexity, more love.

Feel that same impulse—the impulse of creation that has come from the mind of God, that is rising up through all of creation and is now coming through you and me as our own impulse to create.

When we resonate with that inner impulse of creation, it feels like love. It feels like yearning to give every ounce of your gift, of your beauty, of your radiance, into the world. It feels like the *impulse* of God itself, internalized, as your own desire to uniquely express your greater love.

Putting our attention on the feeling of the impulse, let it radiate internally— the frequency of creation as your unique expression of the irreducibly beautiful LoveIntelligence of the Universe through you.

We now dedicate…

- the love in every one of us,
- the brilliance in each one of us,
- the greatness in each one of us,

…to our own unique experience of the process of creation that has created the entire Universe.

KNOWING GOD AS THE GREATEST LOVE OF YOUR LIFE

We enter into prayer.

We enter into the place of prayer.

We do our prayer meditation because we are here to evolve church, to evolve prayer, to evolve *love*. We come to speak dangerous words. We ask that you listen dangerously.

- Are we willing to work with the word church?
- Are we willing to be dangerous and work with God?
- Are we willing to actually participate in the evolution of God?

We talk about the three faces of God. We are laying down new tracks, a new universal grammar of Spirit, and a new evolutionary God language because language creates and reveals Reality.

We have to lay down a new language, to pour new wine into old flasks, to receive old words and give them new meaning—which is the great way of Spirit and its evolution.

We talk about prayer specifically. We don't avoid prayer. We don't call it affirmative prayer.

Prayer means that **we are bowing in devotion before the God who manifested us.**

And who is that God? Is that the Santa Claus God in the sky?

Is it the God that is wholly outside? Is it the God who demands obedience from us with a kind of imperious, divine two-year-old willfulness?

We don't think so! The god you don't believe in doesn't exist.

God is the God who is:

- The Infinity of Intimacy.
- The Infinity of delight.
- The God who knows my name.
- The God who's the power of personhood that lives between each of us—in our personal intimacy that participates in the larger divine intimacy of Cosmos.

We realize that the Divine is not only the Infinity of Power, as the great traditions said, but rather the Divine is the Infinity of Intimacy; **we are God's unique intimacies**.

So, we bow before the Infinity of Intimacy that knows us, that needs us, that loves us, that adores us, that desires us, that holds us.

That is God in the second person, the second face of God.

It is a second-person relationship.

God in the first person: We have the God that lives in the first person—*Tat Tvam Asi, Thou art that. Tat Tvam Asi*—God which is the divine LoveIntelligence, the Outrageous LoveIntelligence that initiated all of Reality. That evolutionary impulse which is shimmering love that lives awake and alive in me, as me, and through me. That's God in the first person.

God in the third person: The evolutionary impulse animated by Outrageous Love, the love that is not mere human sentiment (that's *ordinary* love), but Outrageous Love—the heart of existence itself.

God in third person is the Outrageous Love, the love that drives the Cosmos, the inherent ceaseless creativity of Cosmos—as the great physicist Stuart Kauffman likes to refer to the impulse of Reality.

When we pray, we pray *as* God. We pray *to* God. We bow *before* God, as Rumi does in every poem. Rumi says, let me fall into the arms of the Beloved—God in the second person.

And we know that God is also the force that drives the Cosmos—God in the third person.

THE INFINITE POWER OF COSMOS

Here is our meditation, friends: This is the first time we have ever done Evolutionary Church—there is no second time. The second there is a second time, we are dead.

It is like the first time—every single time. Madonna got it right—*for the very first time*.

To be a mystic is to know this moment is new—it has never been before. This moment is not extra. This moment is pregnant with Divinity. **It is pregnant with possibility because God is the possibility of possibility.**

- We are showing up.
- We are becoming.
- We are waking up.
- We are growing up.

Here is our meditation. We shut our eyes for a second—when we shut our eyes we imagine God in the third person, and God in the third person is the Infinity of Power:

- The laws of physics, the laws of chemistry, the laws which govern and allow for supernovas to take place. The laws of attraction and repulsion, through the original cosmic, great flaring forth that have driven the evolutionary process.

PRINCIPLES OF A PERSONAL POLITICS OF EVOLUTIONARY LOVE

- The dazzling complexity of mitosis and meiosis that existed before there was a neocortex.
- The dazzling gorgeousness of photosynthesis that all of the labs in the world couldn't create with all the super scientists and supercomputers.
- The gorgeous, infinite, unique, and stunning complexity of Reality as it is. The intelligent, inherent, alive third person of Reality—billions of light years, supernovas of power, brilliance beyond imagination.

Our imagination cannot even grasp or touch the brilliance of mathematical equations. Mathematical equations, imagine them dazzling in front of you in infinite, incandescent math.

All of it—all of that power—nuclear power is but a pale reflection of that ultimate power—that ultimate complexity, that ultimate brilliance, that ultimate beauty. **All of that, in all universes—in the multiverses—is God in the third person.**

Imagine all that God in the third person in this moment—sitting in a chair right next to you, looking at you, knowing your name, desiring you, loving you, holding you, tenderly stroking your hair.

All of God in the third person sitting in a chair—in the second person looking at you, knowing you, loving you, needing you. **That is God in the second person.**

So, now we've invoked, and now we realize—oh, my God!—that is God in the second person. And it is before that God—who knows everything that happens in our lives at every moment, every *holy and broken Hallelujah*—that we cry out, *Hallelujah!*

- *Hallelujah* means praise.
- *Holelut* means drunken intoxication.
- *Hallel* is the pristine praise of the most gorgeous moments in our lives.

- *Hallel* is the most broken moment in our lives. All of it is held by God in the second person—the personhood, the infinite personhood, of Cosmos knowing us.

To live without that is to live blind and not know the greatest love of your life. So, we reclaim God at a higher level of consciousness—not the fundamentalist God who's xenophobic and homophobic but God in the second person—the ultimate Buddha, the ultimate Christ.

Imagine the greatest love moment you have ever had in personhood, in your life. Now, exponentialize it a billion-fold and you've got God in the second person—for whom we sing the praise and offer up our *Hallelujah*.

"Hallelujah," Leonard Cohen. [*See Appendix.*]

Everyone has their *Hallelujah*. And remember, prayer affirms the dignity of personal need.

When we pray, no matter what else is going on in reality, there is nothing else to do. If we are preparing anything else, if we are thinking about anything else now, then we've got no idea what it means to be awake and alive in the arms of God in second person. This means we've never read a Rumi poem, and we don't even know what he is talking about.

God shows up, the mystics say, when we show up regularly.

We show up together, and we come to prayer, and something opens in the gates of heaven.

We are invited to step up. Open the gates!

We pray for the most personal things, the most intimate things. We pray for the personal need in life and for those around us because prayer affirms the dignity of personal need. Then we expand our prayer, pray for world peace, and pray for our president-elect as President Obama did.

We pray for this whole complexity around Obamacare. What would it mean if 30 million Americans lost access to healthcare? How tragic that would be? So we pray that the Republican majority has the wisdom to create a safety net for those 30 million Americans who are watching today to see if they will be able to get surgery in 6 months from now.

We offer our prayers.

Remember, everyone, pray your personal prayer. Never skip what you need personally—what you most personally yearn for—and from that personal yearning you can find the yearning for all the Cosmos. If you skip the personal for yourself, you skip the deep prayer for the world.

When we pray we ask for everything.
Prayer affirms the dignity of personal need.

CHAPTER THREE

FROM POWERLESSNESS TO SACRED ACTIVISM

Episode 13 — January 20, 2017

TUNING INTO THE IMPULSE OF CREATION

I am coming to you with gratitude for the healing and the potentiality of the evolving species that is here now on Earth, **where the sacred story of evolution has an expression through each of our hearts**, that sacred story of evolution that carries billions of years of genius in it.

Wherever we are, whoever we are, whenever it is, it is always *on*.

We, in that sense, are always *on*.

Tune into the impulse of creation within us, in our resonance, in preparing for this planetary birth, this planetary awakening, this inaugural of the next stage of human evolution.

Tune in now. Breathe deep into the impulse. Allow it to speak within you, as to what is being inaugurated now, in you, as you, and into the politics of Evolutionary Love. Carrying the astonishing frequency of creativity into the Field of Love, awakening through the irresistible force of creation, guiding us to fulfill the potential in each of us, for the sake of the good of the whole.

We are taking the great traditions of our culture and **deepening it to be the emergence of the new human and the new world.**

PRAYERS TO THE POWER OF DEMOCRACY

We must have gotten sixty or seventy emails this week from people who said they would be at the march in Washington, where the president was inaugurated and people were protesting the president. Both of those are beautiful. Let's hold that beauty as we enter into prayer.

Let's understand, where are we?

- We are in an epic, historic undertaking.
- We are in Bethlehem.
- We are at a crossroads in history.

We are delighted that people were protesting yesterday, and we are delighted that people are at the inauguration because that is democracy. That is how democracy works.

I'm with Barack Obama—and Barbara is with Barack Obama—in wishing President-elect Trump the very best term, even as we are offering our prayers to those who are protesting.

Yes! Yes! We are in this place where we are offering prayers on all sides. **Because there are no sides, there's a greater evolutionary impulse.**

- We are standing against those who demonize the protesters and make them *the crazy liberals*.
- We are against those who demonize the people who are with Trump and make them *the crazy, alt-right conservatives*.

Because actually, we're all Outrageous Lovers: we have the evolutionary impulse of love awake and alive in us.

There's no question in my mind that Barack Obama is right, that President Trump in his deepest place wants to be the greatest president that he can be and not only because of distortions of ego. President Trump may have distortions of ego and so may President Obama, but actually, deep down, the highest President Trump that wants to emerge, wants to create prosperity for the whole world, wants to be a president for the entire country, wants America to be a force for the good. We are going to protest, *and* we're going to stand *with* him because that is the American way; that is the greatness of democracy.

I want to offer our prayers now to President Al Gore who became president but didn't quite get elected. I remember being at the airport, at Kennedy in New York, and Al Gore was giving his concession speech. I was in tears, tears were flowing down my face because that was democracy in action. He had won the presidency, he thought that the Bush team had rigged the Supreme Court vote, but democracy was greater than anything else. Democracy!

We are offering our prayers to the power of democracy.

We are going to offer a new vision of democracy because democracy is not a static, eternal, Platonic form.

Democracy needs to evolve.

What would synergistic democracy look like? What would democracy based on a Unique Self Symphony look like?

We're going to talk about principles of the politics of a personal Evolutionary Love and how we are personally implicated in these politics. How does our actual life—our move from loneliness to loving and awakening—shape and change democracy?

We're about to enter into prayer, friends. What is prayer? We're evolving prayer. One of the reasons President Trump won this election is because the liberal world forgot about prayer. What I mean is, the liberal world got so lost in talking about Spirit as the force moving through Reality. But the liberal world forgot the teaching of the great traditions, which is a beautiful, gorgeous teaching that has nothing to do with fundamentalism.

It's the teaching of Rumi. Remember Rumi?

Rumi is *the arms of the Beloved.*

Rumi is the LoveIntelligence of Reality that:

- Manifested the most sophisticated forms of mathematics, before there was a neocortex.
- Manifested, mitosis and meiosis, before there was a human being.
- Manifested photosynthesis, before there was any supercomputer.

The wild, infinitely gorgeous LoveIntelligence of Cosmos that is personal. The quality of personalness that exists between us, that quality of personal intimacy, that is not just us. That is the *us* participating in the Infinity of Intimacy, which is the divine Reality that knows our name.

Physics, chemistry, the laws of science, and the billions of light-years are all the third person of Reality. That is *God in the third person*: the infinite power, supernovas, and all of the greatest mathematical formulas that guided the Apollo spaceships to the moon, working within the principles of Reality with infinite power, infinite time, and multiverses mediated inside.

We shut our eyes. All of that Infinite Power is sitting in a chair in front of us right now and saying, *I want to know you.*

REALITY YEARNS FOR US

Reality yearns for us. Reality has a personal face that's more personal than any one of us. Imagine your most personal moment with your most intimate beloved and exponentialize that moment billions of billions of times, and you will have the sense of personal, infinite love that Reality has for you.

When fundamentalists talk about it and say, *Christ knows you*, they're actually right. They might be wrong about saying it only using the name called *Christ*.

- Rumi has a different name. Rumi said, *The Friend loves you*.
- Kashmir Shaivism has a different name. It talked about the personal face of Shiva and Shakti embracing you, and Rama and Sita.
- Kabbalah in Judaism has its own words.
- Meister Eckhart in Christianity has his own words.
- The native traditions have their words.

It is the infinite personal face of Reality that knows us, that holds us, that desires us.

Every place we fall, we fall into God's hands. That's why we sing *Hallelujah*. Because what *Hallelujah* means is *hallel*—pristine praise.

Holelut, is part of our ritual, is the drunken intoxication. *Holelut* is the drunken intoxication of our lives in their broken moments. And then the holy moments, the pristine moments, the gorgeous moments, but all of those moments are *Hallelujah*.

All of those moments are held by the Divine. All of those moments are happening within the Divine who cares about the infinite details of our lives. God's there with us every moment.

God knows our name, so we sing before God.

"Hallelujah," *Leonard Cohen* [*See Appendix.*]

It's a cold and it's a broken Hallelujah. There is no one who doesn't know moments of a *cold and broken Hallelujah*, as well as moments of ecstasy. We offer it all up to the Mother, Ramakrishna. Ramakrishna, whose student Vivekananda started the parliament of world religions, Ramakrishna would walk into the ashram and say, *Mother! Mother!*

What do you think? That he was premodern, that he was a fundamentalist? He wasn't a fundamentalist. He just said, *Oh my God, I offer it all up to the Mother.* The Mother is the creative LoveIntelligence that holds us. He would scream, *Mother! Mother! Mother! Mother!*

> *Mother, carry me.*
> *A child I will always be.*
> *Mother, carry me*
> *Back to the sea.*
> *The river is flowing—*
> *Growing and flowing*
> *The river is flowing*
> *Back to the sea.*

The sea, the ocean, is always the Goddess, the *Shekinah*.

Because we look at the ocean for the same reason that we look at a beautiful man or a beautiful woman, just *because*.

We're all beautiful. You can look at anyone's face and fall in love.

- *Fall in love* doesn't mean I'm going to sleep with you or I'm going to marry you.
- *Fall in love* means I see your infinite beauty, you're gorgeous, I'm delighted.

We turn toward the Divine, the creative LoveIntelligence, which physicist Stuart Kauffman called **the incessant, ceaseless creativity of Cosmos in evolutionary science. Which has a personal face, which is** *Mother!*

Let's offer our prayers to Mother. The gates are all open. The gates are open, my friends.

We get to be excited. We are not politically correct. We are spiritually incorrect. We are evangelists—evolutionary evangelists. We are bringing the good news that the evolutionary impulse is alive. And there's a politics of personal Evolutionary Love that's about to be ushered in.

Everybody wants to express their creativity, but most people close their hearts because the pain is too overwhelming

> *Mine eyes have seen the glory of the coming of the Lord.*
> *He is trampling out the vintage*
> *where the grapes of wrath are stored.*

We want to celebrate two people, and then celebrate that very same impulse in us.

Think about Gandhi and Martin Luther King.

Think about how Gandhi, in India, was able to sit and sew and think. He was able to gain the awareness that by doing that Salt March, guiding people to go across India, to be hit, to be destroyed, to be hurt, that he would liberate India from the British.

Let's get inside of Gandhi, for a moment.

What did it take for that small man to stand up, walk across India, have people follow him, have them put in jail, have so much destruction, and win liberation of India?

We are tuning into the spirit of Gandhi and *truth force*.

It is so much stronger than anything in the world.

Now tune into Martin Luther King, standing at the mall in Washington, with hundreds of thousands of people in front of him. He was going to make a speech he prepared. He wasn't sure exactly what to say when somebody pulled the speech away from him. Some friend, who was standing behind him, said, *Just talk, Martin.*

What did Martin say? He said, *I have a dream.* He had a dream of equality. He had a dream of Blacks and Whites living together.

He had that dream, and look what happened. From that dream, that power, and that presence holding that dream, came a Black president of the United States.

We have enormous empowerment of people of color as well as people who are white.

We remember from Gandhi and Martin Luther King, *I am going to liberate India,* and *I have a dream.*

Let each of us experience that unique expression of our gift to the planetary birth, of our unique sound and note, going within, to state it internally first.

Take the lid off the top of your potential. Literally take the roof off the top of your head. You're literally going to allow the impulse of evolution, for the billions of years that it took to get to be in you, by your *Yes*—by your triumph—to actually be heard all the way up.

Let's feel into the same organizing capability that organized the entire universe, the invisible process of creation, that brought quark to quark, electron to electron, proton to proton, all the way up and all the way down the process of allurement.

Let's let everybody's unique gift to the planetary shift be given now as a symbol and an experience of how this can be a planetary awakening of humanity, as a living expression of divine intent.

Take the lid off the top of your head, allow the impulse of evolution to go all the way through, up into the planetary connectivity through the Unique Self Symphony.

We are inviting everybody on Earth to express their gift to the planetary awakening, people in every culture around the world asking the Universe to allow them to give their gift all the way through.

The Unique Self Symphony moving toward a planetary awakening. We feel ecstatic when we are doing that!

A collective planetary birth of what's good, what's true, what's beautiful, then everyone on Earth, people in every culture, all around the world, asking the Universe to allow them to give their gifts, the whole way through, simultaneously.

We are the heralds of the planetary birth.

Who's conducting the symphony?

The same conductor who originated the universe!

The incredible conductor who did those first two seconds of the Big Bang. Now that conductor is a great conductor, as you can imagine!

We are encoded with the Big Bang. We are encoded with fifty-two trillion cells that have been through the entire journey of evolution, that remember what happened.

That's how they do eyes, ears, and thumbs.

How do you suppose they know how to see, hear, and speak?

They are all—the entire body of cells and every one of us—conducted!

The organizing capability that's conducting you is actually also conducting the Unique Self Symphony.

We want to declare a vision that is potentially completely as true as Gandhi and Martin Luther King, and in fact, even more obvious. Here it is: **Every single person on Earth wants to express their creativity.**

Every single person on Earth wants, in some way, to be able to realize their potential self. However they name it, whatever description they give it, it is life force itself, in everyone.

In our Unique Self Symphony, let us all hold together, that this particular symphony is orchestrating what will be, potentially, a planetary awakening in love, in our lifetime, before we have to go into further dissolution and destruction on this planet.

This force is as strong as the Big Bang. This force is as strong as the life impulse of billions of years.

Let's call on it. Let people shout out, go the whole way with your voice.

Feel it the whole way. Let the lid off!

If we take the sense of what the Unique Self Symphony is, while simultaneously every single person is giving their gift, then what actually begins to happen?

Let's understand it:

- What is our response?
- What is our dream?
- What is our vision?
- What is our response to where we are in the world today?

We are spiritually incorrect. Imagine tens of millions of people in the world who all know: *I am a Unique Self; I am a unique expression of the Outrageous Love.* People wake up with a phrase in their minds, and they say, *We live in a world of outrageous pain. The only response to outrageous pain is Outrageous Love*—which is the sutra, the verse.

IT IS NOT YOUR JOB TO HEAL THE WHOLE THING

I am an Outrageous Lover, and I can commit Outrageous Acts of Love that no one who ever was, is, or will be, other than me, can commit, which are a function of my Unique Self, whether I'm in China, in Asia, in Bulgaria, in Idaho, in Canada, in New Zealand, whether I'm a thirty-year-old, a fourteen-year-old, or a seventy-year-old:

- What is my unique contribution?
- What can I do?
- What is my Outrageous Act of Love?

When that happens, when that's in the source code of Reality, then all of a sudden, all of those Unique Selves join and become a Unique Self Symphony.

Our response to President Trump is: we love you, be a great president. But it doesn't depend just on you, President Trump. We are the Unique Self Symphony, the world of citizens, a bottom-up, self-organizing universe.

This is the core realization of evolutionary science and complexity theory rooted in the English mathematician Alan Turing's classic essay, "Morphogenesis." Turing tells us that there are fundamental notes of music—simple first principles of life—that generate reality. I realized when I first came across Turing's *Morphogenesis* that **the simple first rules are not only rules of exteriors, they are also simple first principles of interiors.** These are the simple first principles and first values that animate and guide reality. These are the fundamental musical notes that generate the Unique Self Symphony.

It is not a top-down world dependent on a single separation, an ego-driven leader, or President Trump. Rather the job of the leader is to be the maestro of the Unique Self Symphony.

So, if this is true, let's open our hearts and get really quiet; it's so deep, it's so beautiful, it's so gorgeous. We're not disturbed, we're excited, we're awake, we're alive! Here's the question.

WHY ISN'T EVERYONE OUT THERE DOING IT?

If everyone has a unique gift, and everyone is a Unique Self, and everyone has a unique set of Outrageous Acts of Love to commit, then why isn't everyone out there doing it?

- Why isn't everyone who believes in his vision at the inauguration cheering on Trump or at the protest?
- Why did most people not vote?
- Why are people disengaged?
- Why are people not committing their Outrageous Acts of Love?
- Why are people not stepping up to play their instrument in the Unique Self Symphony?
- Why are people not addressing the unique need in their unique circle of intimacy and influence?

Open your hearts with me. It's so deep. Most of the enlightenment teachers tell us people are not out there changing the world because they are selfish, because they don't feel, because they are egocentric, or because they are narcissistic.

But we don't think that people stop giving their gift because they don't feel. We don't think that people don't show up to the Unique Self Symphony because they don't feel.

The opposite is true.

The reason people don't step up and play their instrument as sacred activists, expressions of Mother in the Unique Self Symphony, is because they feel too much.

They're overwhelmed. They don't know what to do. The suffering is so overwhelming, the problems are so overwhelming, the carnage is so overwhelming.

Yesterday, President Trump talked about the carnage in America. Carnage is a poor word for a president to choose. People are overwhelmed by the carnage all over the world. People say, *It's too much for me! I can't handle it.* People close their hearts. People are afraid to *feel* the pain because they don't know how to *heal* the pain.

---

*In the gap between our ability to feel and
our ability to heal, we close our hearts.*

Get that? In the gap between our ability to feel the pain and our ability to heal the pain, we close our hearts. We close our hearts because we are paralyzed. There's a global action paralysis. There's a global action paralysis because Unique Selves all over the world are afraid to join the symphony. Because the carnage is so great.

President Trump's word, "carnage," is a bad choice because it evokes not our potency but our impotence. *Oh my god, I can't heal it*, is how we respond to carnage. So, if I can't heal it, it's too painful to feel. You've got to hear this; this is so important.

Here's where Trump gets it wrong.

You see, when we close our hearts because we say the gap between our ability to feel and our ability to heal is too great, that's actually just the ego talking. It is not our job to heal the whole thing.

It is our job to play our instrument, to address the unique need in our unique circle of intimacy and influence.

President Trump got it wrong when he said, *I'm the strong leader. I'm going to heal the carnage.* President Trump, we love you, and we wish you a great presidency. But we're not going to be healed by the strong leader. We are past the age of the dictator or the strong president-leader, who is going to actually heal us. We're past the age, and this is where we disagree with the fundamentalists, where Jesus comes only from the outside.

Jesus Christ holds us, but Christ lives in us. We are Unique Selves. We can give our gifts.

Trump is not going to heal the carnage. The self-organizing universe that we talked about before, the maestro, the conductor, is the LoveIntelligence of Reality that knows our name and lives as us. **Each of us has the ability to heal some of the pain that no one else that ever was can heal.**

- Every single person has a unique creativity.
- Every single person has a unique voice.
- Everyone has a unique gift.

WHEN WE CLAIM OUR POWER, WE CLOSE THE GAP BETWEEN OUR ABILITY TO HEAL AND OUR ABILITY TO FEEL

We claim our potency, our power.

We want to say something wildly unpopular for a second: Women and men, we have to claim our power in every arena of life.

- Women, stop being victims.
- Men, stop being victims.

We are powerful. We are potent. We are strong. **When we claim our power, we close the gap between our ability to feel and heal.**

We do confessions of greatness. We hear each other and believe that the process of evolution itself is orchestrating through us. We begin to see that that process created a whole Universe.

We believe we discovered how to orchestrate the Unique Self Symphony: we have to do it together.

We're learning to orchestrate, each of us, such that the chorus that will be heard like Gandhi going on the Salt March and Martin Luther King's, *I Have a Dream* speech.

We're not just watching the movie *Selma*[5] about Martin Luther King; it is us!

This is our turn.

CONFESSING OUR GREATNESS

We don't confess only our shortcoming and our vulnerability. Yes, we have to confess our vulnerability, but we confess our greatness.

We stand before the *lord of song,* and we cry out *the holy and the broken Hallelujah.* By offering up not just the holy, but the broken *Hallelujah.* Love is not a victory march, *it's a cold and it's a broken Hallelujah.*

We offer up all our failure. And all our falling. And every moment that our heart broke open.

And from that place. When it's all offered up to the Mother:

- We find our strength.
- We feel our gift.
- We feel our goodness.
- We feel our power.

We close the gap between our ability to feel the pain and our ability to heal the pain.

We become great players in the Unique Self Symphony. Because **the great principle of a personal politics of Evolutionary Love is Unique Self Symphony.**

YOM KIPPUR STORY OF YANKEL

We end with a story and a chant together. But this story is everything.

Here is the story.

> It's about a Master. This Master knows, he can see, and he understands everything. One of the great nondual Masters.
>
> There is a student that comes in to him on the holiest day of the year. In this particular Hasidic tradition, it was Yom Kippur, the Jewish Day of Atonement, but it could be a Sufi story, a Confucius story, or a Christian story.

Here's what happens. A man comes before the Master, and the Master says, *Get out of here! You're going to die!*

The man said, *What do you mean, I'm going to die?*

The Master said, *Get out of here, you're going to die! Leave me!*

The man was devastated: *That's not politically correct, telling me I'm going to die. You're throwing me out?*

The man was completely broken. He leaves the town, and he's trudging on the road. It's the eve of Yom Kippur, the holiest day in the Jewish calendar and a day of fasting. And he sees a wagon full of disciples of his Master, who are on their way to visit the Master for the holiday.

They say to him, *You look so dejected, Yankel. What are you doing?*

Yankel said, *The Master saw me. He said I was going to die, and he threw me out!*

They said, *Wow, he told you were going to die, and he threw you out! Well, we've got to get a meal before the holiday because it's a fast day. Come and get a meal with us.*

So, what could Yankel do? He'd been thrown out by his Master, he's about to die, his Master told him. He has nothing better to do, so he gets on the wagon, he goes with the disciples, and they go to a local tavern.

The disciples said to him, *The Master said you're going to die. We're right before the holiday, buy us all a drink. After all, you don't need your money, you're going to die.*

Yankel is so depressed and dejected that he says, *Okay*. He buys everyone a drink, and they raise their glass. In the Jewish tradition people say, *L'Chaim*, which means *To Life!*

So, everyone raises their glass. Raise your glass. *L'Chaim! L'Chaim* means *To Life!*

So, the disciples raise their glasses on the eve of the holiday, even the dejected disciple who has been told he's going to die. They raise their glasses and say, *L'Chaim*! They drink it up.

So, everyone, inviting you all, raise your glass, *L'Chaim*!

> Then the disciples say, Pour us another round, after all you don't need your money. The Master said you're going to die.
>
> They pour another round, they raise their glasses and go, *L'Chaim*! To Life!
>
> And they drink up. They pour another round, they raise their glass, *L'Chaim*! To Life!
>
> They drink up, they keep pouring rounds, and they keep screaming out, To life! *L'Chaim*! To Life! Until they're all together in a holy community. A band of Outrageous Lovers crying out, *L'Chaim*! To Life!
>
> Then they're a little drunk, a holy and a broken Hallelujah, and they find their way again to the Master. The holiday is about to begin. The Master sees this disciple that he had just thrown out and said you are going to die. He looks at him, and he says, Oh my god, the angel of death has left. You're going to live!
>
> The disciple says, Master, what happened? Why didn't you give me a blessing? You could have given me a blessing, you could have made me live.
>
> And the Master said, No, there's no guru, there's no Master. No individual can do it. The only thing that can give us life is when we all come together as a Unique Self Symphony, and we raise our glasses, and we cry out, *Hallelujah*! *L'Chaim*! To Life!

We offer it up, and we say that it does not depend on President Obama or former Secretary Clinton. Nor does it depend (as we offer him, as Obama did, our best wishes on his inauguration) on President Trump.

It depends on us!

- We are the Unique Self Symphony.
- We are the Outrageous Lovers.
- We are the ones we've been waiting for.

So, we raise our glasses together, inaugurating a new period in human history in which the center of Reality is not a top-down Reality, but a bottom-up, self-organizing universe, a band of Outrageous Lovers.

We're excited. We're bringing the good news. The good news is us! Because we are alive, and we are awake!

CHAPTER FOUR

EVOLUTION'S DESIRE FOR SYNERGISTIC DEMOCRACY

Episode 14 — January 28, 2017

AWAKENING A MEMORY OF THE FUTURE

We bring into our consciousness the sacred Story of evolution. **The sacred Story of evolution is the guide for understanding the next stage of our lives because there is no reason to assume that evolution stops here.**

Another way to say this is that you and I are called by a deep memory of the past—and a deep memory of the future.

The memory of the past in each of us, when we awaken it, goes back to the origins of creation. Even further, it goes to consciousness itself. The memory of the past in each of us goes to value itself.

Gaining our memory back to the origins of creation allows us to feel:

- every molecule,
- every cell,
- every part of our brain,
- every expression of the trillions of cells that are making us up, that are alive to this memory.

We are bringing into actual form of consciousness that memory of the past as an intentional story of ever higher consciousness, freedom, and order.

Get in touch with the evolutionary impulse:

- toward more life,
- toward more love,
- toward more creativity within you,

...and amplify it.

In this resonant field, take a deep breath of remembrance that we are the story of creation come alive, consciously creating the next stage of self, social, scientific, and spiritual evolution.

We are welcoming the whole story of creation—as you and I—awake to the genius of the process of creation.

FINDING THE FIELD

The Lakshmi[5] chant is a great Hindu chant, and it enters into the interior faces of the Cosmos. It finds the vein of prosperity, the vein of abundance.

I wonder, how did those old-time Hindus, the Kashmir Shaivites, come up with this sacred technology? There was no supercomputer. There was no artificial intelligence. They did not have access to all musical permutations and a Pythagorean array.

How did they do it?

They did it by getting deeply into the resonant Field, feeling the resonance of the Field.

---

5 The word Lakshmi is derived from the root word *laksha* which means goal or objective. To take a *laksha* means to take an aim. The Lakshmi Mantra is recited in order to know your goal and as a means to fructify that goal. Lakshmi Mantra is also called Money Mantra. But Lakshmi Mantra is a prayer not only to gain financial prosperity but also to give the intelligence to enlighten the minds with understanding. Lakshmi is the personification of all that brings good fortune, prosperity, and beauty.

There's noise around us. We can't find it. We are glancing over at a cell phone; we are glancing over here; we are glancing over there. We are disturbed.

If we are asking ourselves, *what's coming next?* Or *what's coming up in the next hour?* We aren't able to find the Field. When we find our way in there, then we can drop in. That is what we have to do here.

The second we are out of the resonant Field, it becomes just a program we are doing. We are not building a program here.

- We are in Bethlehem, friends.
- We are in Jerusalem.
- We are evangelists in the sense that we are bringing the good news.
- We are not just evolutionaries, but we are evolutionary evangelists.

Our colleague, Michael Dowd, wrote a great book called *Thank God for Evolution*. What Michael meant was—and Michael and his wife, Connie Barlow, have been evangelizing for evolution—we stay in.

We are in, committed all the way to bringing the good news.

We can bring the good news, my friends, only if we know the good news. We can feel the interior face of the Cosmos only by dropping so deeply into the silence, so deeply into the presence, that our own sense of presence and radical commitment is so apparent, deep, alive, committed, and true—that everyone can feel it.

The mystics tell us that the second our attention goes to something else, that we are not present, that we are not in; the heavens literally feel it. We focus our attention such that nothing else exists.

Eternity resides in that focus of a radical evolutionary moment.

Our good friend Richard Alpert changed his name to Ram Dass. The Jewish people, they do that. There's Ram Dass, there's Krishna Das, there's

Surya Das, all these Jewish boys from the cities became the Das brothers. Amen, *Hallelujah*. So, the Das brothers, one of the things they were looking for was: Wow, man, let's drop in. Let's be love now.

Let's *be here now*.

Do you see the paradox? There's nothing else, just right here. We are here together in radical intimacy. In radical love.

THE EVOLUTIONARY GOD IS THE IMPULSE OF EVOLUTION AND THE BELOVED WHO HOLDS IT ALL

We are evolving God. We are reclaiming the Possibility of Possibility.

Martin Luther King, together with his great colleagues, could not have started the civil rights movement without one institution—the deep presence of the Gospel church.

It was the animating Eros, presence and delight of the prayer of the Gospel church that carried the civil rights movement.

The deep presence of the African-American Gospel church was the source from which Martin Luther King went out from Selma, Alabama to Montgomery, Alabama, with the Student National Leadership Council.[6]

We are now at the next great movement in history. This is as great as the Renaissance. We are redefining our worldview.

We are stepping up as evolutionaries, understanding…

- that a new world spirituality is emergent,
- that we are evolution awakening as us, in person,
- that the evolutionary impulse, or what Aurobindo called *the evolutionary imperative*, is alive and awake in us.

---

6 On 25 March 1965, Martin Luther King led thousands of nonviolent demonstrators to the steps of the capitol in Montgomery, Alabama, after a five-day, 54-mile march. Source: Selma to Montgomery March in the King Encyclopedia of Stanford University.

We understand the great teaching of Abraham Kook.[7] Kook says, *What is more perfect, that which is perfect or that which is perfecting?*

Ahh, of course, someone who's born with a silver spoon, they've got everything, they were always refined and noble. That's lovely.

But do you remember that movie, *Slumdog Millionaire*, the Indian movie about a man who came from the deep darkness of Reality and managed to transform into nobility? That is perfecting—that is higher.

If perfecting is higher than perfect, and God is perfect, then God must be perfecting; God must be evolving.

So, we pray not to the old Santa Claus God pulling strings from the outside. We pray to the evolutionary God, and the evolutionary God is not only the Impulse of Evolution—

- The evolutionary God is—what Rumi talks about—the Beloved that holds it all.
- It is the impulse that emerges out of the Beloved.
- It is the second face of God.

Let's weave it together.

When we do resonance, we are invoking what we might call the third face of God—the evolutionary impulse, the Field of Evolution.

We always start with the Field. That is the resonance.

Then, we go to prayer.

- Prayer is the second face of God.
- *Prayer is God as thou*, said Martin Buber, *God that knows my name.*
- Prayer is the arms of the Beloved into which Rumi falls,

---

7 The venerable Rabbi Abraham Isaac Ha-Cohen Kook (1865-1935) was the first Ashkenazi Chief Rabbi of Palestine and considered one of the greatest philosopher-mystics of the tewntieth-century.

> *knowing that wherever I fall, I fall into the arms of the Beloved.*

Blessed are you…You…YOU!

There is no place to go, there is no place to be, there is no place to get.

We are taking a stand as ourselves, committed and participating in the evolution of love.

We tell prayer stories. This story is about a master named Levi Isaac Berditchev. There's a formula for blessing in Hebrew, and the formula is *Baruch ata Adonai Eloheinu melech ha-olam: Blessed are you, God, King/Queen of the World.*

Levi Isaac Berditchev was the greatest non-dual mystic who ever lived, at least in the nineteenth century. He was wild, and he could never get through a blessing; he just couldn't do it. A little seven-year-old can make a blessing, but he could never make a blessing.

Why?

Because he would go *Baruch ata… Blessed are you… You… YOU!* And he would start convulsing, and then he would faint in ecstasy.

Because he felt you!

Any intimacy that we feel is participating in YOU, the personal face of the Divine. The Infinity of Intimacy knows our name and cares about every detail of our life.

And, Barbara, I (Marc) am going to tell you a little secret, love, just between us, and please do not share. Yesterday morning, God was worried because you were a little dizzy in the morning. And you felt better, but literally—does everyone get this—the Infinity of Power was a little worried because

Barbara woke up a little dizzy. And thank God, she's fine now, and of course we can all get a little dizzy. But God was like, *oh my god, what's up with my Barbara?*

That wasn't the Santa Claus God.

That was the **Infinity of Intimacy** that:

- Yearns for Barbara-ness,
- Intended Barbara-ness,
- Desires Barbara-ness,
- Needs Barbara-ness.

That realization brings us to prayer. We turn to that Mother, to that You, and we pour out our prayers and say *Hallelujah*. We bring everything. We bring the holy, and we bring the broken *Hallelujah*.

We go into the hymn and prepare ourselves to open up for prayer that affirms the dignity of personal need. We open up with the dignity of our prayer, offering up *the holy and the broken Hallelujah*.

"Hallelujah" — Leonard Cohen [*See Appendix*]

PRAYING FROM THE PLACE OF THE LONELY CHILD

We go from this place into prayer. We know that an evolutionary movement that bypasses *the holy and the broken Hallelujah* is not a kosher evolutionary movement.

Any theology, any spirituality, that ignores the lonely hearts, that ignores the broken hearts, that doesn't understand the shattered place is not a kosher theology or spirituality.

There is not one of us who doesn't know the pain of a broken heart. There is not one of us who doesn't know the pain of betrayal, whether we were betraying or being betrayed. There is not one of us who doesn't know that *love is not only not a victory march, but it's sometimes a cold and a broken Hallelujah.*

And the original word *Hallelujah,* in Hebrew, is *hallel,* which means pristine praise, and it's *holelut,* which means drunken intoxication.

When we go to pray, we come not from the place of the brilliant evolutionary; we come from the lonely child. We come from the one who's throwing ourselves into the arms of the Mother. The Mother who is the LoveIntelligence of all.

Rama Krishna, the great non-dual mystic 150 years ago, when he would go into his temple, he would just cry out, *Mother, Mother, Mother!!!*

And The Beatles got it right when they got the power of *Mother Mary comes to me, speaking words of wisdom, let it be.*

We are praying to the personal face of the Beloved—the Infinity of Intimacy that knows our name. Prayer affirms the dignity of personal need.

ANNOUNCING SYNERGISTIC DEMOCRACY

> *Mine eyes have seen the glory*
> *of the coming of the Lord.*
>
> *He has trampled out the vintage*
> *where the grapes of wrath are stored.*

What does it mean to have a democracy of all?

In the United States of America, this win/lose structure has shown up to be the divided states of America, in order for one side to win over the other.

Think of what it was like before we had democracy. People lived like serfs, people had no names, and the monarchy could boil somebody in oil to see who was right and who was wrong. It wasn't even considered that every individual would have life, liberty, the pursuit of happiness, and the right to vote.

Let us make a deep prayer of thankfulness for the pioneers that liberated democracy to begin with—in the United States, in Europe, etc.—and how great that period has been in terms of liberating individual creativity and potential.

And we are recognizing that the structure of win-lose democracy through voting—great as it was for its time—cannot coordinate us for a planetary sense of connectivity, wholeness, oneness, and liberate the creativity of ourselves when we join.

We have hit a structural impasse because the win/lose structure in all existing liberal democracies is not working.

We are a seedbed for evolutionary democracy. That seedbed is a dharma that is growing in the consciousness of the people. If the Black gospel church made it possible for Martin Luther King to speak *I have a dream*, and his dream was so great and so clear that it was realized to some extent, we are making it possible to state this dream.

Let us be the dream of the next stage of democracy, of the liberation of individual potential, to create a world equal to our divine destiny.

In the particular frequency that we have set, we announce the origin, fulfillment, and dedication to synergistic democracy.

I think we have to ask, what is the synergistic democracy being announced here, whose text is the sacred story of evolution?

In announcing this seedbed of synergistic democracy, we take in the sacred text of the Evolutionary Story as the Evolution of Love.

Feel the awesome generation of capacity that we have—the move from *I* have a dream, to *We* have a dream. The new structure of synergistic democracy is the Wheel of Co-Creation.

THE WHEEL OF CO-CREATION IN SYNERGISTIC DEMOCRACY

The essence of synergistic democracy is built on the win/lose voting structures that gave us the first ideas of individual freedom.

Synergistic democracy starts with the phrase *I want to create*. This is what I want to create.

This is what is my unique passion to express, to give, to become. I want to create.

The second thing that we say in synergistic democracy is: *What do I need to create this better than I could do alone?* The minute we ask each other this, we create our WeSpace, where we can create together for the glory of the evolution of God.

So be it! Here we are in synergistic democracy, and every member of the evolutionary democracy will think:

- First: This is what I most want to create. Whatever it is, my Unique Self is yearning to create it.
- Second: What do I most need, to help me create it, vocationally?
- Third: What do I most want to give freely to everyone because I love to give it? Do I want to give my music? Do I want to give my healing? Do I want to give my humor? Do I want to give my love to caring for children? Whatever it is, I want to give it freely.

Imagine for a moment that the new structure of synergistic democracy is the Wheel of Co-Creation 2.0.

Democracy, as every other human endeavor, has a human structure upon which it was built. The parliamentary procedure is the structure upon which win/lose democracy is built.

Synergistic democracy is built on something that we are all beginning to do, called rules of synergistic order.

What are those rules of synergistic order?

First, when I say, *I'm yearning to create something, and this is what I need*, instead of voting for somebody to create something I don't think is any good, somebody in the evolutionary democracy is going to come to me and say, *I have a creative input to help you create what you want to create*.

Then, by me joining vocationally with you, within synergistic democracy, I am going to get to be more of *who I am*.

In other words, we cultivate vocational arousal in the synergistic democracy of people:

- Choosing what they want to create
- Saying what they need to create it
- Having others join them to create it

Let's say you have entered into the Wheel of Co-Creation 2.0 in the field of health, and you have a new healing process that you'd like to have known. In order to do that, you might say, *I need media attention directed towards what I have to offer*.

Is there someone in the media section of the wheel who has what I need in order to help me create it? Someone is going to say *Yes*, and then you'll have a vocational connection.

You'll experience the joining of genius to create because the person who is helping you will also need you to help them get what they want.

> *We start to cultivate social synergy, coming together to co-create. It is a very natural tendency. Win/lose voting is not as natural as joining together to co-create.*

We had to go through win/lose democracy so that each individual could feel, *I am significant.*

We have come to the end of our ability to be significant as individuals winning or losing alone. In sponsoring the evolution of synergistic democracy, which is the destiny of the politics of Evolutionary Love and follows the great story of evolution as a Love Story, there is an incredible coherence.

We are adding into the synergistic democracy the evolution of our network of communication, our noosphere, our planetary nervous system. We call for it within our communities. We hold small gatherings, we call them *Syncons*, short for "synergistic convergences."

We have wheel-like gatherings in the backs of churches and in small universities—anywhere we want to connect people to co-create.

Within this domain, we are now seeing the development of the next stage of democracy, a politics of love.

We are going to be calling on the genius of the noosphere and all the young tech guys.

And finally, we are going to be calling on the Office for the Future, which holds the Wheel of Co-creation within it and which carries us through, right to the United Nations of this world.

THE DEMOCRATIZATION OF ENLIGHTENMENT: EVERY UNIQUE SELF IS NEEDED BY ALL-THAT-IS

Synergistic democracy, social synergy, a Wheel of Co-Creation. We call this wheel, or what emerges from this wheel: Unique Self Symphony. We call this Wheel 2.0.

In Wheel 1.0, we have the leading innovators in their field. We connect the leading co-creators and innovators of what is working worldwide. We connect them, and that is the first wheel, and that is the elite, which is the leading edge.

But then there is a second wheel that we developed together. We realized that the leading edge is wherever you are.

We have realized that every Unique Self is, by definition, a leading edge with a particular gift to give, a poem to write, a song to sing, and a life to live that is needed by All-That-Is.

Because, once we get Chaos Theory, Complexity Theory, and Systems Theory, we get that it is not about elites.

- It's about the democratization of genius.
- It's about the democratization of superpowers.
- It's about what we like to call the democratization of greatness.
- It's about the democratization of enlightenment.

We say that in Wheel 2.0, you are the leading edge in precisely the right Story, at the right place, at the right time, with the specific and unique gifts to be given, that can be given only by you.

YOU'VE GOT TO TAKE A UNIQUE STAND

The transition happens when we awaken as a Unique Self.

We sat yesterday with John Hanley. John Hanley and Werner Erhard are really the fathers of the human potential movement. John Hanley started what was called Life Spring, a huge movement all over the world, all over the country. What he is really about is taking a stand.

He comes from a place that says something like, *Life is empty and meaningless, and the fact that life is empty and meaningless is empty and meaningless. So, therefore, take a stand.*

Your life is about taking a stand. It's so beautiful: it is the stand that you take.

That is half the story. He got exactly half the story. Meaning, **all the narratives we are telling, all the stories we are telling about our wounding, all the stories we are telling about our hurt, they're all true, and they're empty and meaningless.**

Let it all go. Deconstruct all the contractions of your separate self, and in that emptiness, take a stand. That's step one.

Step two is: You've got to take a *unique* stand. It's a stand that no one else but you can take.

For instance, the reason I (Marc) can be in devotion to my beloved whole mate, Barbara Marx Hubbard, is because I'm not supposed to be Barbara Marx Hubbard. It's not my job; it's not my story. Therefore, I can delight in utter ecstasy and devotion as Reality is having a Barbara Marx Hubbard experience.

And, Barbara Marx Hubbard is not supposed to be Marc Gafni. It just wouldn't work. So, Barbara can say, *Oh, my God, we have these twin evolutionary impulses,* but we don't fuse together—**we join in union.**

We are whole mates looking together at the future, at a shared vision, and that's where the Eros is, and we begin to say, *Oh, my God, I am not willing to be written in the book of life without you. I am not willing to go without you. I cannot do it myself.*

We come together in Unique Self Symphony.

That which unites us is so much greater than that which divides us. We live in one world. There is one love in one world.

> *We are all part of that one love; we are unique expressions of that one love, and we are here to take a stand. We are going to take a unique stand.*

We take that stand for that which is our unique gift, but we take it, not individually, not by ourselves, and not because we were at a foreign meeting and said, *Okay I'm going to take my stand*. We take it as part of the Unique Self Symphony, as our contribution to synergistic democracy. Then we have heaven on Earth.

We have heaven on Earth, and that's just the beginning.

MOVING BEYOND ORDINARY LOVE TO OUTRAGEOUS LOVE

We are going to pray for love. We are going to pray for love together, for what love is. We all want to know what love is.

- We want to know what love is!
- We want to move beyond ordinary love, and we want to feel Evolutionary Love.
- We want to move beyond ordinary love, which is a strategy of the ego.
- We want to feel Outrageous Love as we live in a world of outrageous pain, and the only response to outrageous pain is Outrageous Love.
- We live in a world of outrageous beauty, and the only response to outrageous beauty is Outrageous Love.

I Want To Know What Love Is. This is also a chant that made its way into culture, and everyone thought it was this sweet, lovely, little moment that was purely personal.

But actually, it is the cry of evolution itself. It is the cry that says,

I want to know what love is.

I want to know what it means to awaken as an Outrageous Lover.

What it means to be an Evolutionary Lover.

I want you to show me.

I want to feel what love is.

I know you can show me.

That's the prayer, so let's hold it in this second, and let's open ourselves up to that space, which is Evolutionary Love. And, here it comes, take it away.

"I Wanna Know What Love Is" — Foreigner [*See Appendix*]

Everywhere, we are feeling the deep yearning in the human heart for more love; it goes so deep into the heart. This is the yearning that when we can express it with each other in a field of synergy, it gives the possibility for the God-self to emerge the whole way. In other words, we say the joining of genius creates the new world, the new humans.

The joining of genius creates the opportunity for God to express more fully through the joining of those in love.

YOUR UNIQUE RISK IS WHAT MAKES YOU ALIVE

Evolutionary Church is not Barbara Marx Hubbard, and it's not Marc Gafni.

Evolutionary Church is this *we-space*.

Evolutionary Church knows that the next Buddha is also a *sangha*.

Evolutionary Church knows that we are a band of Evolutionary Lovers.

Evolutionary Church knows that we are willing to take our unique risks.

And, Barbara, we've come together, you and I, to take a unique risk and—at the very edge of evolution—to grow newer, to stand for integrity, to stand for love, and to open our hearts again and again and again.

What we are inviting everyone to do, and you are inviting us to do, and what we're inspiring each other to do, is to be your Unique Self—and to actually take your unique risk.

Your unique risk isn't reckless, fearless, or easy. Your unique risk is what makes you alive.

I am going to tell you a little secret. Everyone's going to tell you not to do it, but there is a unique risk that is yours to take, where you stretch beyond your comfort zone and beyond being comfortably numb.

- For some people, it might be adopting a child.
- For another person, it might be taking a stand in public culture.
- For a third person, it might be giving up being right in your argument with your spouse. Even though we know you are right, but you are just going to give up being right and open your heart just because.
- For someone else, it might be to write the book that you've always wanted to write.
- For someone else, it might be not to write the next book.

Whatever it is, there is a place where you can wake up and be an Outrageous Lover. And you can give a gift of Outrageous Love that all of Reality needs, all of Reality yearns for, and when you wake up to your unique risk, you realize, oh my god, your deed is the evolutionary God's need.

Your deed is God's need.

EVOLUTION'S DESIRE FOR SYNERGISTIC DEMOCRACY

We are delighted, and we are ecstatic, and the word is good, and we feel Evolutionary Love moving through us, and we feel the deep yearning of evolution.

Allurement all the way up and all the way down—living, alive, and awake in us—yearns to create heaven on Earth.

Evolutionary Love yearns to invite Donald Trump to be—as our president—his highest and best self. We invite him, and we give him our radical love.

And we serve the greater good: we serve synergistic democracy.

Let us proclaim freedom throughout the land. And the word is good and all obstacles are melted away. And remember, there's nothing more whole than a broken heart.

The cosmic and the evolutionary merge with the intimate and the personal because they are one.

We bow to and praise the Evolutionary God.

CHAPTER FIVE

OUTRAGEOUS LOVE IS EVOLUTIONARY LOVE

Episode 15 — February 4, 2017

FEEL THE FORCE OF OUTRAGEOUS LOVE WITHIN

We are here as an expression of Outrageous Love or Evolutionary Love. We start Evolutionary Love with the origin of creation. We start it with the orgasmic burst of energy that comes from God. Allow that orgasmic burst.

- Think of its power.
- Think of its genius.
- Think of its intention.
- Think of its animation—of everything that was, is, and will be residing in our hearts.

We allow that orgasmic burst of the Creator force of the Universe to rise. We see it going through quarks, to electrons, to protons, through cells, multi-cells, animals, humans—and us on planet Earth.

We feel that erotic outrageous impulse. We feel God's love for the whole creation. It comes directly into the heart, animating with a force that is truly the incarnation of the divine creative force itself.

Take a moment to experience the force of Love within ourselves—animated by the original love of the creative intention of the universe as us— bringing that intention into our hearts as the animating force of Outrageous Love.

Take a moment to bring that love to our nearby loved ones, our children, our mate. Then animate that ordinary love with the deeper part of what is from Evolutionary Love—love them with that Outrageous Love.

Let love go to them, to the beloveds of the beloveds. Let it spread out to the Universe.

Within a few minutes, by loving those who you love and letting the Outrageous Love of the universal intelligence flow through them, we have reached most people on Earth because **at the heart of Love is *that* force.**

We are here to emanate *that* force in ourselves and reach out into the world in every way that we can—personal, political, social, and scientific—to imbue all that we touch with this Outrageous Love. We feel and announce to the entire force of creation and the entire universal process:

We are here for you;

We are here for Outrageous Love;

We are Outrageous Love incarnate.

Find, in your process of creation, a partner with whom you choose to join in Evolutionary Love and to create the greatest possible future for all of yourselves. Join with that partner and let the Outrageous Love from the origin of creation come directly through you, all the way.

We are here to proclaim, unpack, exclaim, and delight in the articulation of a personal politics of Evolutionary Love. We are here to lay the groundwork for the personal politics of Evolutionary Love—together.

What is the difference between ordinary love and what we call Evolutionary Love or sometimes Outrageous Love?

This is a deep teaching. It is beautiful. It is profound. It is the change that changes everything.

The source of Outrageous Love is no less than God Himself/Herself.

GOD AS THE MOTHER WHO NOURISHES US

First, the god you don't believe in doesn't exist. The God we are speaking of is not the small god. **It is the Evolutionary God: the incessant, ceaseless, creative Eros of Cosmos, moving and yearning towards ever deeper levels of complexity.**

The inside of complexity is consciousness, and the inside of consciousness is Love. Our great Hindu friends call it—*sat-chit-ananda*.

- *Sat*, being.
- *Chit*, consciousness.
- *Ananda*, bliss, love.

Feel it for a second: *Sat* is being; *chit* is consciousness; so the inside of being is consciousness.

The inside of consciousness is *ananda*—love.

Capital "L" Love, Outrageous Love, Evolutionary Love is the Inside of the Inside.

We call it in mysticism, *lifnai v'lifnim*, the Inside of the Inside.

It is *Kodesh ha-Kodashim*; it is holy of holies.

It is *umka d'umka*; it is the deepest of the deep.

We turn to the Evolutionary God who is Outrageous Love, the Evolutionary God who sources all love in Cosmos.

We throw ourselves in devotion at the feet of this Evolutionary God, Mother, because the Mother holds that energy of Outrageous Love.

It is not the mother that you went to therapy about. It is not the mother that you got confused about. It is the Mother who is the Source Mother. It is the Mother who nourishes all and creates all and then destroys all in us that is grasping, small, and contracted. The Mother, who is *Kali*,[8] who loves us in her destruction, to break us open to her.

LET EVOLUTION MOVE FORWARD

When evolution does not move forward, or for instance, when a liberal world does not articulate:

- a new vision of politics,
- a new vision of obligation,
- a new vision of responsibility,
- a new vision of delight,

…when a liberal world only develops all of its teaching around victimhood and does not articulate a new positive vision, when postmodernism deconstructs all of reality and doesn't reconstruct reality, then evolution stalls.

---

8   Editor's note: Over time, Kali has been worshiped by devotional movements and Tantric sects variously as the Divine Mother, Mother of the Universe, Principal energy Adi Shakti. Shakta Hindu and Tantric sects additionally worship her as the ultimate Reality, or Brahman. Source: Wikipedia

When evolution stalls, it regresses.

When it regresses, Donald Trump gets elected president.

Do you get what happens?

Our invitation to Donald Trump is to be an Outrageous Lover. Our invitation to Barack Obama is, come back, be with us, and be an Outrageous Lover.

Let's articulate, together, a politics of Outrageous Love and a politics of Evolutionary Love. We begin by reclaiming God.

Not the god you don't believe in, not the *Santa Claus* god.

Not the *little* god.

Not the grasping god, but the God who is the source of *All-That-Is*.

IMAGINING THE THIRD FACE OF GOD

We are going to do a mediation. Here is how it goes:

We are laying down tracks in the culture itself. We are laying down tracks in the Divine. We are God, speaking within God. **We are participating together in the evolution of God.** We throw ourselves at the feet of the Mother. When we shut our eyes, we imagine what we call this wonderful distinction in the great traditions, **the third face of God:**

> All of the light years of creativity,
>
> All of the creative power of the Universe,
>
> All of the infinite, dazzling complexity and gorgeousness of the *creatrix*, expressed in the table of elements, in the mathematical formulas of calculus and physics, dazzling beyond imagination in their beauty,

Supernovas, which are but pale reflections of the Infinity of Power, which is Reality exploding in every moment,

The laws of mathematics governing every action and reaction in Cosmos,

Power, beauty, complexity, goodness, and dazzling, super, wild, insane, infinite, gorgeous genius beyond imagination…

…*all* of which is the third face of God.

We realize that the infinite third face of the Divine is sitting in a chair right in front of us, madly loving us, knowing our name, and saying, *I want you. I desire you. I love you. I care for you. Receive me, and I receive you.*

And that very God says:

- I want to hear every word you have to say.
- I want to hear your holy and broken *Hallelujah*.
- I want to hear your open heart and your broken heart.
- I want to hear every detail of your life.
- I want to hear every pain and every loneliness, every joy and every ecstasy.
- I am here to hold you.
- In every place you fall, you fall into my arms, and I, Mother, am always here.

This is not the fundamentalist God owned by a particular religion, xenophobic, homophobic, and used for political gain.

This is not that God, but God who is the Infinity of Intimacy, sitting in a chair in front of us, yearning to fulfill, to meet us, to love us open into our highest most gorgeous self, to hear and receive every *Hallelujah*!

Let's hear the Goddess, receiving and singing *the holy and the broken Hallelujah.*

Let's impress on the lips of God, *the holy and the broken Hallelujah.*

PRAYER AND SEX ARE THE SAME THING: YOU CAN'T PRETEND

Prayer affirms the dignity of personal need. Prayer says that every *holy and broken Hallelujah* matters. Prayer says that we may live lives of quiet desperation.

Even if there is only one set of footsteps on the beach, we never live lives of lonely desperation. When we are in pain, we are being carried. We are being held. Every time we fall, we fall into the arms of God.

If we allow the personal face of essence, the personal face of Cosmos that knows our name, to be hijacked by a regressive, fundamentalist meme that says, *we own it. Only Allah, only Christ, only the Jews, only the Tibetan Buddhists*—If we allow evangelism to *bring the good news only of fundamentalism*, then we forget to say, *thank you, God, for evolution*. We forget to claim the evolutionary God that lives, alive in us and knows our name. We forget to be *evolutionary evangelists*.

We are evangelists. The new word of evangelists is the good news of evolution.

The good news is held in every moment. Every need matters.

We offer our prayer. Our prayer is not just for peace in the world. It is for peace in the world for every animal and every plant, but it is also for Uncle Morris, who is having an operation.

To pray, you have to find your child-self. You can't be in your sophisticated self.

Prayer affirms the dignity of personal need. Pray for everything.

Be willing to let go of ego, and throw yourself before the Divine Mother, who knows your name.

If we do not feel personal needs coming through here, we are not yet praying. We cannot bypass personal need. **If we don't have personal need, then we don't love ourselves.** We've got to pray for personal need. To pray, we drop the ego.

The mystics say prayer and sex are the same thing.

When you sway back and forth in prayer, the *Baal Shem Tov* says, it is because you are sexing with God in both prayer and sexuality.

You have got to drop your ego. **You can't pretend. You've got to let the raw truth of you come forward and impress that truth, that depth, that gorgeousness, on the lips of God.**

Feel prayer rising. Offer prayer for everyone. Let the prayer roll. Let the God times roll. Let's not be afraid to drop our ego and fall down on our knees in devotion before the Mother. Blow it open, and love it open.

Let us set the tracks for an evolutionary God awakening in us.

A TASTE OF PLANETARY CONNECTION

It is outrageous. I want to pick up greatness and share what I know is happening, **through each of us as we express our unique greatness.**

Something happened to me (Barbara) this weekend when we had a high-tech summit here in Sunrise Ranch. These were people who are very sophisticated with the internet, in community building, and other kinds of talents who look as though they might be separate from this deep and personal love we are feeling.

I had a moment there; it was quite late, and I said, while talking to all these different high-tech geniuses, *would you like to know my internal experience of the Planetary Awakening in Love?*

Well of course, they couldn't say no! They all had to hear, *how does a planet awaken in Love through each of us?*

I started by saying the first thing we felt—and **I am saying this as though it already happened**—was outrageous pain. And as you know, the alternative to Outrageous Love is outrageous pain and not just a little bit of pain—major pain.

The human species, for one moment in time, felt the pain.

All of us.

That was the key to the beginning of the birth. It was very similar to a physical birth.

It is when the pain is the worst, when you are giving birth to a baby, when you say, I cannot stand it anymore, that something new can happen.

Right there, what I saw happen was that the outrageous pain instigated empathy in humans.

As we often do, if we face an immediate crisis, we become heroic, but usually, the empathy does not last, and the pain continues. In this moment, I am sitting with these high-tech people, and I said, *How would it be possible for there to be mass empathy?*

This would be the fulfillment of the politics of love.

I said: *Is there anybody here who would know how to cultivate mass love?*

So one man, Richard, stood up and said: *I can!*

I said: *What! Are you joking? Tell me. How can you? I am talking for real. We have a planetary crisis. We need to have mass empathy to make the shift. How would you do it?*

With the tremendous love in his heart—the love of innovation, creativity, and talent at a high level—he drew me a diagram of how, in a community, there are connections made out of our own interests. Those connections lead to more connections, which lead to more connections. He said: *Within a few days you could have many connections, leading to more connections, leading to more connections so that there would be a field of connectivity. That would be mass empathy.*

I said: *Alright—Let's do that! I mean, instead of just looking at it as a possibility.*

When I said, *this is necessary for God to be able to emerge as a Planetary Awakening, starting with empathy*, these talented people became part of our team. The next thing I declared was: part of the awakening is exactly what we are doing here—we began to hear, in our own voices, the inner words of God.

We are preparing for a birth. When each of us feels from within this inner voice, we want to be connected.

Everybody wants to be connected. We know that the way nature works is by allurement, by attraction—electrons with electrons and protons, all the way on up. We are doing what comes naturally.

Human society has forgotten it.

The next thing I declared is that there would come a time out of the mass empathy when there would be a mass experience of the inner voice speaking in everybody's own language.

How does God speak if you happen to be a Christian, if you are Chinese, if you are Jewish, if you are from Ethiopia? How would God speak to you? In your own language, obviously, and in your own terminology that means something for you! This was a planetary Pentecost, which I am realizing is a future forecast.

The First Pentecost came to the disciples of Jesus, who were in the upper room after his crucifixion. They were afraid they would be crucified themselves if they appeared anywhere, but they gathered anyway. What happened was, the Galileans, who were speaking in Galilean to groups of different languages, had gathered in what they call, the upper room.

Somebody said, *how is this possible? The Galileans are speaking one language, but we are all hearing it, in our own language?*

Peter got up and said, *This is what has been prophesied by the Prophet Joel: In the last days, God will pour Spirit on all flesh, simultaneously. Your old men will dream dreams. Your young men will see visions.*

The Second Pentecost is when all the various people on Earth, like ourselves, heard in our own language the inner communication of the Outrageous Love of God. It came out in all the languages. In this experience, what happened was, the walls of religion fell down.

They had only been there, the walls of the religions, until we could all hear it, in our own language. If you don't hear it in your own language, if you don't hear it from within, then you need the help. Our hope, our prayer is that the walls of separation fall down.

The next thing that happened was really exciting. In the old days, it was called the media. The news began to pick up the stories of people totally inspired and healed, like when Jesus walked through a village, people got healed. How did that happen? He was filled with unconditional love—the people were so in love with this inner voice that they were healing each other. You see, I am putting it in the past tense.

When sitting in this room with these high-tech people, I started to say, *the media would be able to pick this up, as people are healing and hearing the inner voice.* Some of the high-tech people, Adam Apollo and Harlan Wood, stood up and said: *We can be that media! We know how to do a distributed network. Anybody who places their gift, their prayer into this network will be connected with others.*

Then, more media started to come in and say how they could find each other by vocation. It started to go quantum. For me to realize that the talent is all here was delightful. They need to be invited into the new story of the evolution of the Divine.

I was able to give a birth story at that conference, not expecting what would happen, but what did happen was that the twelve people who said yes to this formed a new team, then everybody wanted to be part of this team. They are still here at Sunrise Ranch, working. People are coming in, from far and wide, because there is a notice. The word has gone out. We are going to do this. This is for real.

Each of us has a talent that comes from God.

We are orchestrating something here that has not been orchestrated before. By being together at our sacred retreat, we will have time to orchestrate the notes of the Unique Self Symphony that each of us hold.

We will have a taste of a planetary birth experience.

We will have a taste of a planetary Pentecost.

EVOLUTIONARY LOVE IS OUTRAGEOUS LOVE

Friends, let the symphony begin. Let's take the next step. In order for the symphony to begin, we have to lay down the tracks this month, to allow for this planetary birth experience, what Barbara and I love to call **the Planetary Awakening in Love through Unique Self Symphony, the planetary awakening in Outrageous Love.**

We need to understand and lay down a new *dharma*, new teachings for this universal church, this universal synagogue to emerge.

It is not to get rid of all the religions. Every religion should practice and play its instrument in the symphony. From the diversity of instruments emerges a world evolutionary spirituality greater than the sum of its parts, which is *ontologically orthogonal* to everything that came before that.

Who knows what ontologically orthogonal means? It means it is something new. It is synergistic. It never was before. It is the newness, incessant creativity of Cosmos, birthing this new Evolutionary Church.

To do so, we cannot be lazy. To do so, we cannot bypass. **We need to lay down the tracks in our hearts of the new *dharma*, of the new teaching that will allow us to have heaven on Earth**. The beginning of that *dharma* is the distinction between ordinary love and Outrageous Love.

Ordinary love is a strategy of the ego. It is fine. It is legitimate. It is okay.

Ordinary love means:

- I am afraid, and I want to be comforted.
- I feel alone.
- I feel like, somehow, I am not going to survive. I want to be secure.

Those are the first needs in Maslow's great hierarchy of needs. Those are legitimate and holy.

That is ordinary love, but ordinary love will not take you home. Ordinary love wanes and fades.

Ordinary love—as it grows older—disappears, dissipates and dissolves, which is why people are searching for love in all the wrong places. It is why we play love songs all the time but feel somehow that we did not make it. How many people feel in this lifetime we did not realize the love we wanted to realize because we are looking for ordinary love to fill us?

Ordinary love comes from the separate-self. It is the grasping, contracted ego searching for comfort, and then we get comfortably numb.

Remember the band Pink Floyd, a few decades back, and their song, "Comfortably Numb"?

We want to wake up beyond ordinary love and find love in its source: Outrageous Love, Evolutionary Love.

Evolutionary Love or Outrageous Love *isn't merely a human sentiment*, said the Bengali poet Rabindranath Tagore. Outrageous Love, Evolutionary Love, *is the heart of existence itself.*

Evolutionary Love is the Evolutionary Eros that allures molecules together.

Evolutionary Eros is the attraction, the allurement, the sacred dance of coming together, which lures all of Reality.

It is the very lure of becoming, said Teilhard de Chardin.

Swallow it into your heart and take it in deeply.

Let your heart explode in Evolutionary Love, as we lay down together these holy distinctions, feel them, and get what they mean.

THREE DISTINCTIONS BETWEEN ORDINARY LOVE AND OUTRAGEOUS LOVE

Let's make some distinctions.

The first distinction:

- Ordinary love is about comfort.
- Outrageous Love is about pleasure.

You get the difference?

Comfort means, I do not want to feel dissonance. I do not want to feel tension; comfort me. Now comfort is legitimate—and a little shot of whiskey comfort is sometimes good to down the pain, but you can drown in that whiskey.

You need pleasure.

The opposite of pain, people say, *is pleasure.*

That is not true. The opposite of pain is comfort. Do you get that? The opposite of pain is comfort.

The opposite of pain is not pleasure because all pleasure incorporates some degree of pain, some degree of breaking open.

> *If I do not break open, I cannot become whole, and there is nothing more whole than a broken heart.*

Outrageous Love says, *I want pleasure*. We live in a society that says, *live as long as you can, as comfortably as you can*. Then, when we get to be 110, we wonder where did all that pleasure go? Wow! We lived so long… *comfort, comfort, comfort*. Nooo, claim your pleasure! And your pleasure comes from embracing all of it—*the holy and the broken Hallelujah*.

Ordinary love—comfort.

Outrageous Love—pleasure.

Let's go the next step.

The second distinction:

- In ordinary love, as a structure of the ego, you are either giving pleasure or receiving it. In ordinary love, giving and receiving are opposites.
- In Evolutionary Love, in Outrageous Love, giving and receiving are the same.

To be an Outrageous Lover is to know that there's no difference between giving and receiving.

We say in the teaching of Outrageous Evolutionary Love that the sexual models Eros, or Outrageous Love.

OUTRAGEOUS LOVE IS EVOLUTIONARY LOVE

In the sexual, to be a great lover, it is not about giving or about receiving; giving and receiving collapse into one. Giving pleasure and receiving pleasure are the same. Wow!

For an Outrageous Lover, an Evolutionary Lover, where I love it open in every dimension of life, there is no distinction between giving and receiving. It is the same thing.

The third distinction:

- In ordinary love, when you give it away, you no longer have it.
- **In Outrageous Love, when you give it away, you have it ten times over.** It is like a flame of light: when you light the candle, then you take the candle and you light another candle. Does the first candle lose any light? Of course not! Because light is Outrageous Love.

We live in a world of "the great deal." My good friend, President Trump, has got Outrageous Love in his heart. He loves beauty. He loves outrageousness. He loves power. He desperately wants to do good for the American people. We are going to love you open, President Trump—appreciate all that is good and wonderful and beautiful.

I have learned so much from you. You wrote a book called, *The Art of the Deal*. The problem with *The Art of the Deal* is, when you make a deal, you are always trying to make *a great deal*.

What is a great deal? A great deal means you got the most, and you gave the least. In that second United States presidential debate, when you were asked about what you paid contractors, you said, *well I didn't always pay all the contractors because I was being a good businessman*.

I get that! You are brilliant in so many ways I couldn't even touch. But, can I humbly offer you this? **In a real deal, an Outrageous Love deal, you do not get the most and give the least. You both give outrageously. There is an ethic of generosity.**

When I hear you talk, President Trump,

- ◆ I feel the generosity.
- ◆ I feel your goodness.
- ◆ I feel your integrity.
- ◆ I feel your beauty.

By the way, I am furious with everybody demonizing you. We have had enough of that. We want you to succeed.

We are outrageously loving you.

The true art of the deal is the art of Outrageous Love.

You give the most, and you receive the most.

And giving and receiving, there is no distinction between them, whatsoever, that is the art of the Outrageous Love deal.

STORY: THE GREAT MASTER OF CHILDREN

Here is a story. It is a break-my-heart story. It is a true story that my teacher told. His name was Shlomo Carlebach.[9] I am going to tell his story in first-person, but it is his story. He was a folk singer and a mystic.

> He tells a story about a great, wise man named Kalonimus Kalman Piaseczno who was this Rebbe, this master of children, who lived in Europe in Piaseczno. This most beautiful man—he was killed in Treblinka[10] in World War II. But before he was in Treblinka, he was in the Warsaw Ghetto. In the Warsaw Ghetto,

---

9   Shlomo Carlebach (1925–1994) was an influential rabbi, singer, composer, and spiritual leader often known as the "Singing Rabbi." He is widely celebrated for his contributions to Jewish music, spirituality, and outreach. Born in Berlin and raised in Austria and later the United States, Carlebach initially studied in Orthodox yeshivas. However, in the 1960s, he began to engage with more diverse Jewish and non-Jewish audiences, spreading messages of love, joy, and connection through his music and teachings.

10   Editor's note: Treblinka was an extermination camp, built and operated by Nazi Germany in occupied Poland during World War II. It was in a forest north-east of Warsaw, 4 km south of the village of Treblinka. Source: Wikipedia.

he wrote a book called *The Holy Fire,* a book that drips with holiness.

He continues,

> I was walking down the street in Tel Aviv. I was by the ocean, on a street called Ha Yarkon Street. I saw a man, a little man, a hunchback. This hunchback was bent over. He was disfigured, but his eyes were somehow shining. He was sweeping the streets.
>
> I stopped this hunchback, and I said, *where are you from?*
>
> He said, in a thick Polish accent, *I'm from Poland.*
>
> *Where are you from in Poland?*
>
> *I'm from Piaseczno.*
>
> *You are from Piaseczno? Did you know the great master of Piaseczno?*
>
> He said, *Did I know him? I was one of his children. He was the master of children, and in his home hundreds in his neighborhood, thousands of children lived, whom he supported.*
>
> *Of course I know him.*
>
> I asked him, *you knew the great master of Piaseczno? Could you give us a teaching from him?*
>
> He said, *can I give you a teaching from my master? Look at my disfigured body. I was five years in Auschwitz, in the concentration camps. The blows broke my body. Do you think I remember a teaching, even from the holy master, after five years of outrageous pain?*
>
> I looked at him, and I said, *you can never forget a teaching from the holy master of Piaseczno because those are teachings of Outrageous Love. Please, please could you remember a teaching for me?*
>
> He put down his broom. He put on his jacket. He put on a tie. He said, *yes, yes, I am going to tell you a teaching. I now remember a*

teaching. Tears were streaming down his cheeks.

He said, *Every Sabbath, hundreds of us would gather in the home of the Master, and he would say a teaching between every meal, between the fish and the soup, between the soup and the meat, between the meat and the dessert. He would sing a chant. And after every chant, he would say a teaching. The teaching was always the same:*

Mayn kinderlach, taire kinderlach—my children, sweet beautiful children, di greste zach in di velt ist zu tun mit emetzin a tova—the best thing you can do in the world is do a favor for someone, no matter what.

He would give a teaching, and at the end of every teaching, he would look at us, the children, and would say, mayn kinderlach, taire kinderlach—dear children always know, di greste zach in di velt—the greatest thing in the world, no matter what is happening, ist zu tun mit emetzin a tova—is do a favor for someone.

I got to Auschwitz, and I was strong. I was 15 years old, said the street cleaner. *They looked at me and they wanted to break me. They started beating my body, that's why I became so disfigured, until I was hunched over. That's why I became a hunchback, my face so close to the ground.*

Do you know how many favors you can do in Auschwitz with your face so close to the ground?

Do you know how many people are dying?

Do you know how many people are broken and lost?

So, I would walk around Auschwitz, and I would listen to every story. I would listen to every person's dying wish. And I would listen to every yearning.

Every time I wanted to go to the electric fence in Auschwitz and throw myself against the fence, I would remember the words of my Master, mayn kinderlach, taire kinderlach—children, dearest children, di greste zach in di velt—the greatest thing in the world, ist zu tun mit emetzin a tova—is to do a favor for someone else.

My dearest, beloved friends, that is not ordinary love. Do you understand? **That is Outrageous Love.**

I was just talking to my friend, Arthur Kurzweil. Arthur just went to Europe. He went to the town in which his entire family was massacred. He found in that town that the tombstones of all the Jewish people had become latrines, toilets.

He went to the mayor of the town, and he said, *would you allow me to take these latrine tombstones and rebuild them into a monument?*

The mayor was such a good man. He said, *yes!*

Then, Arthur said to me, *Marc, I was thinking about that teaching of Evolutionary Love, Outrageous Love, and I heard the words, "We live in a world of outrageous pain; the only response to outrageous pain is Outrageous Love." I heard it flowing in my heart and head and I just spoke spontaneously to the mayor and said, Could I do you a favor?*

The mayor said, *what do you mean?*

He said, *Listen, di greste zach in di velt, the best thing to do, is to do someone a favor. Would you let me do you a favor?*

The mayor doesn't know what he means, and he says, *yes, of course, you can do me a favor.*

Arthur says, *I want to build a playground.*

He didn't say, I want to have peace and reconciliation talks: *I just want to build a playground for all the holy children.*

That is what he is doing right now. He is right now in Ukraine, and he is building a playground for all the holy children in that town, which destroyed his family. Wow!

> *We live in a world of outrageous pain.*
> *The only response to outrageous pain*
> *is Outrageous Love.*

Let us awaken in Evolutionary Church as Outrageous Lovers. Not ordinary love, not a strategy of the ego, but Outrageous Love. Let Donald Trump awaken as the Outrageous Lover that he is.

I am remembering when I tweeted a few weeks ago that *Donald Trump is an Outrageous Lover*. A whole bunch of beautiful adversaries of mine—bless them—retweeted, *how could you say that Trump is an Outrageous Lover?*

Don't you understand, friends? If we demonize Trump, he becomes a demon. It is the same as how the Right demonized Obama; they didn't let him do anything and tied his hands behind his back. Now we're going to demonize Trump? I don't think so. Is Trump an imperfect vessel for the Light? Yeah, I think he is. I think he is. Did I vote for Donald Trump to be President? No, I didn't.

We are speaking to Donald Trump not in a voice of demonization but in a voice of Outrageous Love. Even when we protest, even when we are at a women's march, we are not coming from a place of demonization. **We are coming from a place of Outrageous Love, and we are calling that forth in the world.**

LET US BRING MASS EMPATHY

The outrageous pain, feel that rising up out of Outrageous Love:

- Because of the shared crisis on this Earth,
- Because we are the generation who were told that within one more decade, we could have lost our environment,

- Because we are the first generation to be told that evolution is conscious in us.

What I would like to bless here is the massive uprising of those who *do* love. One more degree of connectivity to those already arising, wherever they may be.

A beautiful last point here: **our crisis is a birth.**

All this separation—and this illusion of separation—that has plagued the human species, I call a "nervous system defect." Somehow, many of us do not feel empathy.

Let's be the evangelical call for the mass empathy, for the mass connectivity of that which is already loving.

Here is my biggest, straightforward insight that I had from God: *There are enough of us now. We are all here, people of every race, creed, color, size, shape, capacity.*

We are filled with one thing alone, the Outrageous Love of God, as our creative expression of Evolutionary Love.

CHAPTER SIX

HEALING THE GLOBAL INTIMACY DISORDER WITH A NEW POLITICS OF INTIMACY

Episode 16 — February 11, 2017

RADICAL PLANETARY INTIMACY

I am coming to you from the Infinity of Intimacy. In order to experience the Infinity of Intimacy for ourselves, let us, for a moment, go into the Infinite. The Infinite is an extraordinary, almost impossible, concept to imagine—in terms of intimacy.

Give yourself evolutionary eyes. See planet Earth as one living body from space. Feel the pain of the entire planet for one instant in time. Imagine the collective pain so great.

Feel the spreading of deep empathy, feel with one another that intimacy at the level of infinity. Breathing into how you feel, when you feel with someone else, deep, deep down—intimately empathic.

Imagine for a moment that everyone who is awake to the yearning for intimacy is feeling it together on a planetary scale as a living organism. Feel that empathy becoming radically, massively experienced as the heart of

our desire being fulfilled on a planetary scale because the heart's desire for intimacy is joining genius.

Joining genes means that we create babies through intimacy. What are we joining in *radical* intimacy and *radical* empathy?

> *In Infinite Intimacy, we join genius through empathy, love, and attraction.*

We are joining the unique genius of each person, the unique vibrational field of that inner impulse that is expressing as you, uniquely.

Experience **yearning in your heart** for union, communion, joining to create.

As in sexuality, ultimately nature's purpose is joining to create a baby; in radical infinite intimacy and desire, our *yearning* is to join genius *to create ourselves*:

- A new human and new humanity
- Our full potential
- *Homo amor*

Our babies are our work—all of us—creating the new planet together. In this moment of radical intimacy and resonance, let's experience radical planetary intimacy, joining our genius and making our work a point of expression of a planetary love. The intimacy of our desire to join leads us into what we have been calling **the politics of Evolutionary Love at the social scale**. This is our resonant field.

THE MISSING TILE SYNDROME

We just heard some distracting typing. Let's use this as a pointing-out instruction for the *Missing Tile Syndrome*.

Imagine, in Castile Spain, in the medieval period, they had to work through persecution, pogrom, plague, the Black Death, in order to serve God.

But we, the challenged privileged, when something bothers us, all of a sudden, we are taken out of our center, and then we focus completely on whatever that thing is that is bothering us and the beauty, the gorgeousness, and the joy that is happening in that moment disappears into the sound of someone typing on the side while someone is talking.

We are okay, we are happening, we are alive, but the core teaching here is that:

Practice is in everything. The first thing you need for intimacy is to watch out for the missing tile syndrome.

The *Missing Tile Syndrome* is very simple: you are living your life, looking up, and you have a thousand good tiles, and they are awesome! But you are missing one tile.

- You have got a thousand gorgeous tiles, but one is missing.
- Your eye moves to that missing tile.
- You focus on that tile.
- All the other tiles recede, and all you can see is that missing tile.
- That missing tile angers you.
- You get upset.
- Then you get more upset and more upset.

Practice is everything.

The nature of being full and alive and intimate with yourself is that you learn not to get taken out of your center.

THE SCROLL OF ESTHER

I'll tell you something wild: there is a sacred text called *The Scroll of Esther*.[11]

In that sacred text, there is a story about a man named Haman, who is second to the king. The king is Xerxes, in the ancient kingdom of Persia where King Darius had been the interlocutor and adversary of Alexander and Philip of Macedon. The second to the king, the *mishleh le'melech* from the original Hebrew text, is called Haman.

Haman has everything.

There is just one dude in the kingdom—that dude's name is Mordechai— Mordechai bothers him. Because there is something about Mordechai's Eros, about Mordechai's authenticity, and about Mordechai's Outrageous Love—whatever it is that makes Haman feel *less*. The text reads: *All Haman can see is Mordechai*.

Mordechai makes him feel *less than*; malice is aroused, and he moves to destroy. He had this desire to annihilate Mordechai.

This entire book, one of the twenty-four books of the sacred canon of the Bible, is about a person getting lost in the *Missing Tile Syndrome*!

We can use the Yiddish word *khap*, meaning "I grabbed it." I gave a little extra *dharma* on the *Missing Tile Syndrome*, about being intimate with ourselves, locating ourselves in our center and not getting thrown out of our center. To be intimate with ourselves goes something like this:

Know that inside of you, there are 75 trillion cells which are uniquely YOU! They are dancing in a dazzling cacophony and symphony of

- biochemical resonance
- electromagnetic resonance

---

[11] The Scroll of Esther, or Megillat Esther, is a book in the Hebrew Bible that tells the story of Queen Esther, her cousin Mordechai, and the Jewish people's survival from a plot of genocide in ancient Persia. This narrative is the basis for the Jewish festival of Purim, celebrated annually in early spring.

- neurological resonance
- nerve resonance
- atomic resonance...

...in a dance, in a cacophony of light, sound, and vibrational impulse that no supercomputer could possibly imagine or produce.

Yet, it was produced as uniquely *you*, by the Cosmos. It is happening—as *you*.

THE INTIMATE KISS OF PRAYER

From that place of gratitude, we pray. We evolve prayer together—we evolve God together. We evolve together. We choose to reclaim a post-postmodern vision of God. We participate in the evolution of prayer—in the evolution of God.

> *The god you don't believe in doesn't exist. The prayer you don't believe in doesn't exist.*

Warren Farrell[12] likes to say, *I believe in prayer*.

What does prayer mean?

I am reminded of a reading from Rumi. It goes like this. Rumi says:

> If anybody wants to know what Spirit is or what God's fragrance means, lean your head towards Him or Her. Keep your face

---

12 Warren Farrell is an American author, political scientist, and activist known for his work on gender issues and men's rights. Initially involved in the feminist movement in the 1970s, Farrell served on the board of the National Organization for Women (NOW) in New York City. However, over time, he shifted his focus toward what he saw as issues facing men and boys, which led him to a more critical stance on certain feminist ideas. He has since become one of the most prominent voices in the men's rights movement, often exploring themes like fatherhood, education, male psychology, and family court reform.

there, close. When someone quotes the old poetic image about clouds gradually uncovering the moon, slowly loosen knot by knot, the strings of your robe, like this. If anyone wonders how Jesus raised the dead, do not try to explain the miracle. Kiss me on the lips like this, like this.

Imagine friends—we are in the intimate kiss—not sexual.

The sexual models the intimate; we are in the intimate kiss of prayer.

- Prayer is when we impress our lips on the lips of God.
- Prayer is when we know that God yearns for us.
- Prayer is when we know that God is not the fundamentalist, xenophobic God.
- Prayer is not owned by the liberals bashing Trump or by Trump bashing the liberals.
- Prayer is not owned by the Jews. Prayer is not owned by the Christians. Prayer is not owned by the Muslims—because God is not a Muslim, a Jew, or a Buddhist.
- God knows what we are feeling because we are intimate with each other. I am close to you. I can feel you feeling, and I am a fraction, a fractal of the Divine.
- God is the Infinity of Intimacy that knows our name.
- The Divine feels our ecstasy.
- God feels our pain. God feels our brokenness. God feels our holy and our broken *Hallelujah*.

God is the personal face of the evolutionary impulse that manifests *everything* before any neocortex, any supercomputer. God is the LoveIntelligence that runs through all of Reality that expresses itself uniquely as us, even as She/He holds us whenever we fall.

This is the God who receives our prayer. This is the God of the holy and the broken *Hallelujah*.

We are here not just to say this to each other, friends. We are here to reset church in the world. We are here to reset synagogue. We are here to create the Evolutionary Spirit of a world spirituality that becomes a new language, a new meaning that binds all of us!

God is talking through us.

God is talking through me.

God is talking through you.

Let's open our hearts in ecstasy as we pray. Prayer affirms the dignity of personal need. Let's pray. Let's cry out our prayers.

I am praying for years and years of holy evolutionary partnership, fucking open the *dharma*, putting beauty and gorgeousness into the world. I am delighted to pray for that.

Everyone, cry out!

Cry out our prayers—our prayers are for ourselves. We cannot bypass our own intimacy.

RADICAL FULFILLMENT OF LIVING YOUR HEART'S DESIRE

Here is radical intimacy and radical fulfillment of our heart's desire. Let's go the whole way in this lifetime with the fulfillment of intimacy and desire.

What is your deepest, most radical, heart's desire? Let it be deep, truthful.

Recognize that **by our intention placed in our heart's desire**—the impulse of evolution in every one of us, which is the heart's desire, is the longing of evolution for more life, more love, more freedom, more greatness—**we are turning on the Unique Self**, the Essential Self in every one of us that holds the power of the billions of years of evolution encoded within it, to fulfill our heart's desire at its highest level.

> *In order for the Universe, for God, to be able to fulfill your heart's desire, you need to desire it.*

The Unique Self desiring its fulfillment *is* the essence of evolution come alive in you.

Here is Maslow's hierarchy of human needs, with a bit of an extension that Maslow himself did not give us.

- There are *deficiency needs*—of hunger, security, loneliness. Our heart's desire is to fulfill those needs.
- There are our *growth needs*—to find our unique expression and creative vocation, powerful needs.

Let us say, at this moment, all of those needs are fulfilled—basically we are not hungry, starving, or in the midst of a war. Many have found some expression of life purpose.

Maslow had—at the third level of needs—*transcendent* needs. We translate the words *transcendent need* to the words *evolutionary need*.

What are the evolutionary needs of our intimate heart's desire as Unique Self? They are expressions of the whole process of creation incarnate uniquely in every one of us! We are the seedbed of the evolutionary impulse of humanity taking off! We are the seedbed of the joined geniuses of humanity's heart's desire.

What is the heart's desire at this most radical, intimate level of joining? Our most radical, intimate heart's desire is for a degree of planetary union that could awaken our planetary body to its collective potential in love.

That does not sound like an intimate heart's desire, does it? There is *a lot* of intimacy included in there. In fact, *everything* I desire is included in there.

But to express it *the whole way*—for radical intimate heart's desire being fulfilled—it is *that* expression on a planetary scale.

In this radical intimacy of heart's desire, can you identify, if you go the whole way with it, to the third level of Maslow's hierarchy of needs to the fulfillment of your evolutionary need—of your Unique Self need in intimacy?

Let's allow our most intimate heart's desire to be God's desire. Let's do confessions of intimate heart's desire, going the whole way in this lifetime. Because if we do not desire this, overtly, do you know what? God cannot fulfill it, intimately.

- Evolution is longing.
- Evolution is yearning.
- Evolution is your heart's desire being fulfilled in this moment.

By joining together, we are joining genius.

That means the frequency of our deepest impulse of creativity, internally, is joining and fusing with each other's genius.

Feel it; we are collectively joining genius to co-create.

WHAT DOES CO-CREATION MEAN?

It means that the creator within you—expressing the unique impulse of the God force, the evolutionary supra-mental genius force inside you—joins with the genius of others.

We know the miracle of joining genes to have a baby—it is totally miraculous.

Out of that sperm and egg comes the beginning, in this little egg, of a heart, a lung, legs and arms. It has not ever seen, walked, or heard, and it is grown in the womb from the joining of genes.

What happens to us with the joining of genius, if so much happens with the joining of genes to have a new baby? **The joining of genius creates a new humanity.**

Do you feel this?

Can you be intimate? What does it feel like?

Let's declare, in the presence of the Divine, that our yearning to join genius creates a field in which the heart's desire of others begins to pulse—like that egg when the sperm hits it.

Oh! If we can allow and feel and invite the genius of others!

We want to move from a global intimacy disorder to the evolution of intimacy, but we live in a moment of global action paralysis. That paralysis is rooted in something deeper: a global intimacy disorder.

> *It is not that we have lost intimacy on a global level… we have never had it. We have never evolved to that place.*

Evolution is no less than the evolution of intimacy—the entire evolutionary process. This is one of the great innovative *dharmic* structures, mimetic structures—to understand that **evolution is no less than the evolution of intimacy itself.**

This *dharma* is our vehicle, CosmoErotic Humanism.

We need to evolve *together*.

We are together evolving the source code.

The evolution of the source code is the evolution of intimacy itself because we have exiled intimacy.

THE EXILE OF INTIMACY

When we think of intimacy, we think first of human intimacy—we think intimacy is a human experience. That is the first exile: only humans experience intimacy.

Then we think that intimacy means a particular kind of romantic human experience—a monogamous, classical, white-picket-fence, dog, man-woman. We think that is an intimate experience. If we are liberal, we allow *man-man* and *woman-woman*. If we are really liberal, sometimes, we allow three people to get together, but that is often the limitation of our intimacy.

Then, we exile intimacy even more when we say that intimate relations are *sexual* relations. We have completely exiled intimacy. But, no, intimacy is much deeper.

We live in an Intimate Universe.

Wow! Can you hear that, my friends? Tweet that out into the world! We need to move from global intimacy disorder to a new order of intimacy—to the evolution of intimacy.

If you want to know why there is a global action paralysis, it is because **shared *action* comes only from shared *intimacy*.**

- There is nothing more erotic than creating together.
- There is nothing more intimate than awakening as a unique incarnation of intimacy that we call Unique Self.
- There is nothing more intimate than participating together in the Unique Self Symphony in which the Infinite and intimate resonance of our unique voices joins in sacred activism to create a genuine sacred America.

Not a top-down "I am the President," but a bottom-up, "We are the people."

Are we evangelists? Yes! *We are evangelists* meaning we are bringers of the good news, and the good news is the good news of intimacy. We are past the place of *the sage from the stage*. We are in the place where we recognize and understand that the next Buddha is a Buddha *and* a *sangha* filled with Buddhas.

Not that there is no hierarchy, not that there is no leadership—there is always leadership. And yet, we are *all* leaders. We are all evolutionary leaders because we are all offering our evolutionary intimacy into the space.

We can do that only if we do it for real, my friends. The second we demonize a person, the second we create a culture of attack, the second we lose our empathy, and the second we get lost, we are in a failure of empathy.

Every second of our lives we are failing in our empathy. We fail in our empathy because it is too painful to open up all the way. We need to break down a little bit in order to break open.

We have to break down:

- The walls of our ego
- The places of being comfortably numb
- The hatred that underlies the self-righteousness and critique of President Trump

Underneath it you feel an invective, which is an anger, a malice that no one wants to identify. There is not just an alt-right; there is an alt-left.

But it;s not a left-right issue. Let us be human beings together. Let's realize that that which unites us is so much greater than that which divides us. Let's realize that right now, as Libby Roderick said to us in her song: *How can anyone ever tell you that you are anything less than beautiful? How can anyone ever tell us that we are less than whole? How can anyone fail to notice that our love is just a miracle and how deeply we are connected in our souls?*

Let's surrender to intimacy. Yes! Because *we want to know what love is.*

Give us the prayer—"I Want to Know What Love Is." [*See Appendix.*]

That is our hymn. That is our prayer.

We are spreading to the world because it is our turn.

It's our song.

It's our prayer.

CHAPTER SEVEN

THE COLLECTIVE AWAKENING OF HUMANITY

Episode 17 — February 18, 2017

ROOT CAUSE OF GLOBAL ACTION PARALYSIS

Together we are holding the *dharma*, the teachings of CosmoErotic Humanism. We are building this as they did in Bethlehem, in Mecca, in Jerusalem, in Asia Minor, and in China.

This is a new moment, particularly in Western history.

We are the ones gathered around the table. We are the disciples. The evolutionary impulse of love is in the middle of the circle.

We are the ones. It is our turn. Let's have a good time, and let's laugh! We know this is our turn. It's the next turning of the wheel.

- We are post-religion, yet transcend and include all religions.
- We are the next emergence in the evolution of love.
- We realize we live in a world in which there is a global action paralysis where people see the suffering and yet do not move to heal it because we do not feel we can impact it; we feel alienated from the whole story, and we feel impotent in the whole story.

The global action paralysis is rooted in a global intimacy disorder. We can *heal* the outrageous pain only if we *heal* the disorder of intimacy. **The global action paralysis is our inability to respond to outrageous pain.**

We have to heal the global intimacy disorder.

We respond to outrageous pain with Outrageous Love. We live in a world of outrageous pain, and the only response to outrageous pain is Outrageous Love—to awaken as conscious evolution.

When we respond to outrageous pain through Outrageous Love, what we are saying is we are reclaiming intimacy.

We are saying—the action paralysis is a failure of intimacy.

The outrageous pain is a failure of intimacy, so we need to reclaim intimacy, and we need to restore intimacy.

There is a loss of intimacy, and a loss of intimacy is when we are not talking face-to-face, we are not feeling each other, we are not in dialogue. We have to be in dialogue with the people we disagree with.

We have to make peace always, with our enemies, and not just with our friends.

Intimacy is feeling you feeling me. If we can:

- Model what it means to talk face-to-face,
- Model what it means to give up being right.
- Model what restoration of intimacy means,

Then we *will* move the needle on the compass.

I am honored, and I am delighted.

I am thrilled to set the resonant field for the planet as we realize *it is our turn and it is time to move the next step forward.*

MEDITATION: ONE EVOLUTIONARY ACT OF LOVE

Let's feel Evolutionary Love, Evolutionary Intimacy.

The question I asked myself this morning was, what is an evolutionary act of love?

Here is a guided meditation in the experience of Evolutionary Love:

- Go within and find a place of hurt or wounding, where you have been hurt or you have hurt another. Feel it deeply. Remember everything about it that you can, experientially, in every cell in your body. Remember how it feels to be hurt or to hurt another.
- Ask it to reveal to you an evolutionary act of love that you can take, on the inner plane, that is only yours to give.
- Let your Unique Self respond fully, deeply, truthfully.
- Feel yourself responding to the hurt that you have received or given, when you are feeling with that other person and yourself.
- Feel the intimacy.

In the process, deepen your own intimacy, feeling the pain you have received or given, intimately. Go deep into it. Go the whole way in. Feel the other's response when you are feeling them intimately, feeling you loving them.

What does it feel like? What happens? What revelations are revealed to you in this act? Feel the intimacy informing you of the process of Evolutionary

Love as you are giving it.

How does an inner evolutionary lover feel? What makes it an evolutionary act of love rather than simply an ordinary act of love? It *reveals* to you that the evolutionary act of love *is* an expression of the *whole process of creation as you.*

> *You are the evolutionary impulse toward greater love, greater freedom, greater wholeness, being expressed through you, by your act of evolutionary love.*

Feel the opening in your heart. Feel the guidance as to how to love more, where it hurts.

Take time in your journal or in your meditation to return to this. Identify the experience of love, where it hurts, and the guidance you receive as to your healing action, your evolving action, your emergence as your full potential self, changing the world in this act of Evolutionary Love.

RESTORING INTIMACY: GOD IS ALWAYS WITH US AND FEELING EVERY PULSE OF OUR INTERIOR.

We move into prayer. Our intention is not only to be more awake and more loving. Our intention is to play the largest game possible, the largest *Divine* play available, to participate together in the evolution of love.

Two questions we ask are:

- Are you ready to play a larger game?

When we say *play*, we mean in the Kabbalistic sense of *sha'ashua*, the original Biblical word, which is Divine play. Divine play is completely serious, ecstatic, and urgent. It has a sense of ecstatic urgency in which there is everything that needs to be done—even as it has deep rest.

- How do we be in ecstatic urgency and deep rest at the same time?

Barbara and I were talking as whole mates—*how do we take care of each other in the urgency and the resting?* It is so tender between all of us, so exquisitely tender. Our theme is evolutionary acts of love. Let's hold it with two *feeling tones*—with ecstatic urgency and with quivering tenderness.

Let's give each other a gift of ecstatic urgency and quivering tenderness, held together. **Prayer is about the restoration of intimacy.**

I listen to gospel songs with a friend. We get on the internet and find different gospel songs from different gospel churches. We do a lot of Elvis because Elvis was gospel—you cannot understand Elvis without gospel. We do Elvis. We do gospel. We are deep in the fundamentalist world.

THE THREE FACES OF GOD

If you go to a good fundamentalist church, you will feel intimacy in a way you do not feel it with Episcopalians and Unitarians—with all due respect—because the fundamentalists haven't given up on the integral distinction we make: *the second face of God.*

The *second face of God* is key to who we are.

But first, we know the first face—*Tat tvam asi,* Thou Art That—which in the classical enlightenment traditions means:

- Essence lives as you.
- There's no self.
- Beyond your personality, you are consciousness.

No, the first person of God is not just *Tat tvam asi,* Thou Art That—we say it is, *Thou art the evolutionary impulse.*

Thou art the evolutionary impulse awakening in you—that is the first person or first face of God.

We have the first person: *I am the evolutionary impulse. I am Essence.*

We know *the third face of God,* which is the evolutionary impulse running through all of Reality.

We feel the evolutionary impulse, this incessant, ceaseless creativity that drives Cosmos in every second, to borrow Stuart Kauffman's phrase slightly amended.

We have lost the intimacy of the *second* person, which is any of us loving each other even when it is hard finding our way to the intimacy.

I want to tell you all a holy, little secret, so gentle. I want to whisper it because it is a *Lechisha De'Orayta,* as we say in the sacred Aramaic texts that inspired Jesus. It is a divine whisper.

To the precise extent that you have had your most intimate moment in the entire world, imagine your most intimate moment, when you felt most close.

God is closer to you than even that.

Can you hear that?

God is closer to you than even that.[13]

> *Lo bashamayim heeh,* He is not/She is not in heaven.
>
> *Lo me aver ha yam,* She is not across the sea, says the holy text.
>
> *Ci-Karov aleicha hadavar meod meod,* She is very close to you, says the sacred text.

She is intimately whispering in your ear, and that is prayer.

The Evolutionary God is not the god you don't believe in. As we are setting the new source code, the god you don't believe in doesn't exist.

We need to reclaim church, reclaim synagogue, reclaim mosque, and reclaim prayer at a higher level of consciousness and know that:

---

13 See Deuteronomy 30:12–14.

- Prayer expresses the Infinity of Intimacy.
- Just as the third person of God is the infinite power of Cosmos, that infinite power of Cosmos is also infinitely intimate.

We live in an Intimate Universe.

God hears Barbara. Barbara and I had an exciting conversation for four minutes last night, as we were in between two things. **As we were getting all excited about it, God was getting all excited about it.** He was probably saying, *slow down kids, slow down*, but it's like this: **Whatever you feel, God feels!**

You know what? Remember *Walden*, by Henry David Thoreau, when he said, *men live lives of quiet desperation?* Well, I'll tell you a secret. There are no lives of lonely desperation; we are never lonely because:

- Christ
- God
- Atman is Brahman
- Shiva/Shakti
- Earth/Sky
- The Infinite LoveIntelligence of Reality that knows our name

…is *always* with us, feeling every pulse of our interior.

OFFERING PRAYER TO THE INFINITY OF INTIMACY

We pray to God affirming the dignity of our personal needs. We know that God is with us.

We reclaim prayer not only for ourselves but to reset the entire Field of Consciousness, as we reunite with the Divine in *unio mystica* and we know that we are intimate.

We are One; God is holding us.

Every place we fall, we fall into God's hands.

God holds and kisses us in the *holy and in the broken Hallelujah*. Let's love each other madly. Let's love it open, *the holy and the broken Hallelujah*. Let's offer up our prayers.

We offer up our holy and the broken *Hallelujah, holelut,* which means pristine praise and drunken intoxication. *Love is not a victory march, sometimes all I've learned from love is how to shoot someone who outdrew ya, but in every moment, in every moment, she is drawing from our lips, the Hallelujah.*

We offer prayer to the Infinity of Intimacy that knows our name. We pray for what we need because if we do not affirm the dignity of our personal need, we'll never heal the need of others.

If we do not feel the Universe loving us madly and feeling our worth, feeling that our needs matter, then we cannot love the person next to us. Do not pray for world peace, pray for Uncle Maurice.

Let's not be lazy before the Divine and say, *I'm not gonna pray.*

Hello, let's wake up! Let's reclaim the power of prayer from the fundamentalist grip which is homophobic and ethnocentric!

Yes! We are evangelists! We are evangelists because it is good news. We offer up and invite the prayer of everyone whose heart is too closed to pray. We *feel the movement,* and we know that the word is good.

We know that all obstacles are melted away, and we know that we get to be excited. We feel quivering tenderness and ecstatic urgency at the same time.

EXPERIENCE A PLANETARY BIRTH IN RESPONSE TO PAIN

Feel the voices of evolution coming up into the field. I am reminded both of the intimacy of the early Christians, personally loving each other in small circles and taking the Eucharist—*this is my body, this is my blood, given for you.* There is nothing more intimate than eating the body and blood of Christ.

Then the vision of the Second Coming, the planet moving towards newness, toward love. This started the entire Western civilization of the evolutionary potential of humanity fused with the great Jewish tradition of giving our gift in obedience to the law. But, as Marc writes in his beautiful *Radical Kabbalah*, **becoming the voice of God, yourself—that is evolution.**

I have been working on the inner meditative state. I have been feeling pain and asking, *how do I also release pain?*

I have found the experience of meditative states to be very powerful and a real expression of what is happening. I share with you an inner experience I would like us to have together. It has guided my life to this very moment.

We know that through each person fulfilling their unique expression and through the planetary body coming together as a whole, we can be in time to save ourselves from the devolutionary shift.

FEEL THE IMPULSE OF EVOLUTION

Place yourself in the shift point on planet Earth. **Feel the impulse of evolution coming through you, toward more being. Not only your own now, but your own being as part of the planet.**

Feel the extreme pain through the whole planet simultaneously. As one body—the wars, prisons, hunger, disease, and separation.

See planet Earth as one living system—one body in pain.

Feel the global paralysis that makes it so difficult to evolve our actions—when we feel the pain to be so extreme that it is *impossible* for any one of us to overcome it.

Feel that now.

In the planetary birth experience, feeling the pain first releases a little empathy here, some empathy there, and then empathy everywhere. The new part is … the empathy does not stop. We remain empathetic as a new state of being, moving towards mass empathy.

Let us feel: what would mass empathy on a global scale feel like *in response* to the pain?

Not just our own empathy—mass empathy.

I (Barbara) remember one experience I had of this was during the end of the Second World War when it was announced on everybody's radio, *the war has ended.* I was in an apartment on Park Avenue in New York City, and I, like everybody else in every apartment, ran down into the streets. There were military, sailors, soldiers, people, old women, young women, everybody started to dance on Park Avenue, everybody started to hug each other, kiss each other, love each other.

It was mass empathy. We felt like one planetary body, a newborn planetary baby held in its mother's arms after the pain of birth. We knew something was being born.

We know that a biological birth is painful. We know as mothers and fathers of that pain, we bring it in. We feel the pain because we know it is the pain of birth. After we feel this pain of birth, this empathy is hearing the voice of Spirit within all of us together, uniquely.

Feel the voice of Spirit uniquely as you in this moment, whatever it is saying beyond the prayer. The voice of Spirit is already actualized. It is already who you are. It is already fulfilled.

- I am Love.
- I am Goodness.
- I am Creativity.
- I am loving the whole world.
- There is nothing left out of my love.
- Let that be so.

Each in our own voices, let Spirit speak from within, not as a religion, not as a dogma, but direct knowing of the Unique Self within, speaking uniquely as you, together with others.

We are heralding the Unique Self Symphony.

COMING TOGETHER IN MASS EMPATHY AND MASS FORGIVENESS

Imagine everybody's voice in mass empathy. What does the voice of Spirit say to you as we are feeling mass empathy, feeling with those who have been hurt, as well as those we have hurt, en masse?

You see, if it can happen individually, if we are one planetary body, it's possible for the planetary body to feel together.

We are penetrating the inner psyche of humanity, feeling all the hurts, wounds, and separations, allowing the voice of Spirit within each of us to hear the voice of Spirit within others.

We can come into mass empathy together.

It cannot be done one culture by one culture, one nation by one nation. In this state of being, it happens simultaneously. Every culture has wounded some other culture. Even the Buddhist cultures have wounded another culture. Every person has wounded and is wounded. Every culture has wounded another.

It cannot be resolved, one by one, through ordinary processes of forgiveness. Let it all go!

Forgive everyone who ever hurt you.

Feel their pain. Feel our mass intimacy, mass empathy, and mass forgiveness. Feel this mass forgiveness.

Mass empathy—feeling with—we are doing it. The nervous system of humanity is capable of connecting us. The nervous system of humanity is ready to have a shared experience of oneness with every one of us in it. It is not only a vision. It is an evolutionary capability of a very young birthing process. In this instant the illusion of separation can disappear.

Why can it disappear?

It is an illusion. We are really not separate.

> *We are not separate from anyone or anything or from the impulse of evolution itself.*

Connect with your heart now through everyone, with everyone again, that you ever hurt or who has hurt you. Feel that inside yourself.

I had a healer who once gave me this process which I want to share with you as part of this forgiveness. She told me:

- Go through everything you can ever remember—when you hurt anyone or have been hurt before
- Go year by year by year.
- Get into your mother's womb and feel it all the way as you were once a little tiny egg with one little beating heart.
- Take that all the way through and come out the other side of your mother's womb.

When I did that, I had this feeling of complete lightness. This was when the word *re-genopause* occurred to me (Barbara). I was not degenerating. I was regenerating.

I was no longer having the eggs. I am the egg. Feel that inside yourself.

What happened?

I found myself out of my mother's womb, completely free of any pain. I was sitting on a ledge with a group of people. It was in Athens at the very edge of Greece, there I saw behind me Socrates, Plato, the great Greek sculptures and temples. Then I heard the words, *Barbara, you are to jump off this ledge with this group of people.*

Let's be the ledge. Let's be on the ledge. Let's be on the ledge together.

Ready? We are going to jump off together.

THE FOUR QUESTIONS TO HELP CREATE THE PLANETARY AWAKENING

I was guided to ask four questions of everyone that would help create the planetary awakening.

- Do you remember having volunteered to be here? Do you remember having volunteered to come to this planet?
- If you do remember—in one sentence, what is your contract? You came in for a purpose, what is your contract?
- What are you meant to do?
- Whatever it is you are doing, what do you most need to do better?

Imagine what you need to do, so that your unique best is given.

Imagine yourself doing it fully now.

YOU CANNOT ENTER INTIMACY HOLDING HATE IN YOUR HEART

These four gorgeous questions are all asking the same thing, which is: **What are the evolutionary acts of love that are *yours* to commit that are needed by All-That-Is?**

Just feel it coming down.

- You are intended by All-That-Is.
- You are desired by All-That-Is.

- You are needed by All-That-Is.
- You are adored by All-That-Is.

Once you know these noble truths in your body, you can answer the great questions.

The new evolutionary creed is emerging.

THE DAY OF ATONEMENT

There is an old sacred tradition, the *Day of Atonement*, the day in the great Western tradition of Mary Magdalene, the day on which all Christian mysticism is based, the day when the high priest enters the Holy of Holies once a year: *Yom Kippur*.

On that day of radical intimacy with the Divine, we forgive each other.

It's deep. You hate one person, then all intimacy is blocked. You hate two people, then even more intimacy is blocked. If you hate one person and there is one person you have not forgiven, then all intimacy is blocked.

You cannot enter intimacy holding hate in your heart.

As we protest, we do not hate, do you get the difference? We have to transform. We have to let the hate go from our hearts. **We cannot bypass doing the personal act of face-to-face transformation to mass empathy.** That is a bypass.

We have got to first let go of the hate in our hearts—with the people that it is hard to do so—and then we can find our way to mass empathy.

That is one-half of the teaching. The other half of the teaching is: *by accessing the mass empathy, it will melt the hate in our hearts.*

It's both.

We cannot bypass doing the personal work to mass empathy, but:

THE COLLECTIVE AWAKENING OF HUMANITY

- We have got to go to the mass empathy.
- We cannot make it all personal.
- We have got to hold it on both sides and let it go.

It was the Grateful Dead that said, *What a long, strange trip it is been!* Oh my god!

And Bob Dylan said, *When you live outside the law, you've got to be honest!* Friends, we are living beyond the law. We are in the law, and we are beyond the law.

We are beyond the law, and we are going to love in every moment. OLATT.

OLATT. *Outrageous Love All The Time.*

What a delight!

CHAPTER EIGHT

THE EVOLUTION OF REALITY IS THE EVOLUTION OF LOVE

Episode 18 — February 25, 2017

NO ONE LIVES A LIFE OF LONELY DESPERATION

In the original Hebrew, eighteen is *Chai*, it is life! Let's revivify our lives. Let's reclaim prayer.

My friend Zak Stein and I like to quote to each other a statement by this great philosopher, Immanuel Kant, who said *the modern person is embarrassed to be caught praying.*

Why are we embarrassed to be caught praying?

Because we understand prayer to be to a fundamentalist, Santa-Claus-like god in the sky, who happens to be:

- A little homophobic
- Totally ethnocentric
- A massive supporter of a more extreme version of reality than Trump

No, the god you don't believe in doesn't exist, and the old vision of prayer is a wrong vision of prayer.

> *Prayer is the affirmation that we live in an Intimate Universe.*

Imagine your most intimate moment with your most intimate friend. In the Intimate Universe, that love, that moment of intimacy, is more than just you and your friend. You and your friend are participating in a Field of Intimacy.

Similarly, when I (Marc) am doing push-ups, I am powerful, but that is not just my power. I am participating in the power of Reality.

A car has more power than my push-ups, and Clint Fuhs, who can bench press way more than I can, he has more power than I do. I can barely lift one weight—Clint does like six thousand pounds. A jet propulsion engine has more power and a supernova has more power.

Our power participates in the power of Reality.

The intimacy between someone and their friend, it is not just them. **They are participating in a Field of Intimacy.** God is not merely—as the great traditions said—the Infinity of Power, God is the Infinity of Intimacy. That relationship between a person and her friend, in its most intimate, participates in this Infinity of Intimacy.

We realize that, in every moment, we are held. And every place we fall, we fall into God's hands. The god you don't believe in doesn't exist. We have got to liberate that experience of the second person of Reality—the Infinity of Intimacy that knows my name—from the *fundamentalist grip*, to understand that in every moment:

- ◆ We are known.
- ◆ We are held.

Men and women may lead lives of quiet desperation, but if you are really awake—if you are really enlightened—**it means you are aware of the**

nature of Reality. No one lives a life of lonely desperation because as the great Hebrew mystics said, *Bekol Tzaratam Lo Tzar,* in every moment when you are in joy, I am in joy with you; in every moment that you are in pain, I am in pain with you.

Whether this is:

- The Christ message, or
- The Buddha message, or
- The Hebrew messianic message, or
- The Lao Tzu message,

...it's the same message: I am with you. I suffer with you. I am in joy with you. In prayer, we bring it all, and we lay it on the altar of the Mother.

Sally Kempton, one of the great teachers of the Divine Mother in the great Kashmir Shaivite tradition, teaches that what we do in prayer is: **We lay it all at the feet of the Mother. Everything!**

Prayer affirms the dignity of our personal experience, *our holy and our broken Hallelujah.* Remember Leonard Cohen, who says, *From your lips, She drew the Hallelujah.* It is all *Hallelujah*! In the original Hebrew, *Hallelujah* means: *Hallel*, pristine, gorgeous order, and praise. And *holelut* brokenness, drunken intoxication, not of the good kind.

Prayer affirms the dignity of personal need. **We pray for whatever we need in the world because we recognize that, in the intimacy of Reality, we wildly matter.**

That is not narcissism. That is an affirmation of our irreducible and gorgeous dignity as Unique Selves. We know that Reality intended us, and that our needs matter. We claim those needs.

We pray for ourselves, every personal need, every person that we know of, and then we expand our prayer.

We pray for the entire world, and we pray for transformation.

We pray for:

- Everyone who does not know that you can pray
- Everyone who thinks that somehow, we are walking in the world alone
- Everyone who thinks that we live in a world which is "a tale told by an idiot, full of sound and fury, signifying nothing"
- Everyone who does not realize that we live in an Intimate Universe

In every moment, I am seen. In every moment, I am recognized. In prayer we get over the affliction of being systematically misrecognized. We realize that we're in a moment in the world where we face a global action paralysis. That global action paralysis is rooted in a global intimacy disorder.

Only by healing the global intimacy disorder will we be able to heal the global action paralysis.

You can't heal an intimacy disorder just by working it out with your one loved person.

You have got to heal it by *restoring the fabric of intimacy* that is at the *core of Reality*.

The Divine, the All-That-Is, the Infinity of Intimacy, yearns for our prayer.

WHEN YOU GIVE YOUR GENUINE GIFT OF LOVE THE WHOLE WAY, THE SUFFERING IS GONE

I have a prayer for America—in terms of overcoming the suffering of the world—**a deep prayer for the evolution of America.** I want to start by noting the enormity of the simple sentence that was stated years ago, *we hold these truths to be self-evident, all people are created equal…*

Look what *that* did. That statement appealed to the ancestors of everyone in the United States of America and beyond. My grandparents (Barbara) all were Jewish, from Austria and Russia. Those were difficult places to have come from in those days. Not everybody from Austria and Russia came over here, but some of them did. My grandmother was sixteen when she came over on the boat. They would not let her off the boat because she didn't have any money. The story goes, she talked her way off the boat! Her husband—my grandfather—was a tailor in Brooklyn. They were *thrilled* to be in America. My father was a poor boy in Brooklyn, who liked dogs, as I remember.

But he did something very American: he was the first person to think of making inexpensive toys. Before my father, only rich people had toys. He teamed up with Walt Disney and made inexpensive toys for everybody. It was very, very American. And, when I asked him—a Jewish agnostic, no religion—what religion we were he said, *You're an American. Do your best.*

So I began to wonder what that could be. What could anybody's best be?

I'd like to rephrase Thomas Jefferson, *We hold these truths to be self-evident, that all men are created equal.*

Let's change it to: **We hold these truths to be self-evident that all people are born creative, not equal necessarily—everybody is born creative. Let's just affirm in ourselves that unique creativity we are born with— given as a gift of the Universe itself, a gift of God.**

The genius of you is creative. All people are born creative, endowed by our Creator.

It is really good to bring your own sense of unique creativity as a gift from our Creator. You didn't make it up. You were given it.

Then, the thank you. Thank you, God, for the creativity.

THE EVOLUTION OF REALITY IS THE EVOLUTION OF LOVE

I am a Jewish woman. I didn't think about that until recently. Marc gave a talk on the Jews and what they are like. The Jewish woman, I believe, is innately designed to give birth to the culture of a compassionate world. So I say *Yes* to that creative gift.

I am born creative. You are born creative, endowed by our Creator with that unique gift. I am capable and responsible—response-able—able to give the unique gift I was given. The unique gift every single person in the world was given to express that creativity the whole way.

The call to express the innate gift given by God—the whole way—as your responsibility.

That does mean you are able to give your unique gift the whole way. **Everybody's creativity is way beyond what you think you can do.**

Take a moment to think of the creativity welling up inside you, and by a gift of God you are response-able—*able* to give it the whole way—and take the lid off the top of your life. Just take it off!

God gave it. Instead of confessing our weakness, we are called to confess our greatness! Who gave it to us? Can you say, *I am response-able to create my unique creativity for the good of myself and all Earth life?*

Is that true? Am I responsible for doing THAT? Are you responsible? When you do that—when I do that—what happens to the suffering in the world? Where does that suffering go—first of all for yourself—where does it go? When you or I say yes we are 100 percent response-able for giving our gift the whole way, what happens to your suffering?

It disappears! It's gone.

The feeling of suffering disappears, but not necessarily when you're in a terrible crisis of illness, war, or disease. Yet, even then, it's possible to overcome suffering through giving your gift. The gift of God inside you—when you give it—provides you with divine energy and love.

You can only give your gift in love. You cannot give your gift the whole way—the *whole* way—without feeling love. The offering of overcoming the suffering of the world is your genuine gift.

When you give it, you are love. When you are love, the suffering goes. Go into love. Let's give our gifts with love as the way to heal suffering.

We refuse to dismiss suffering as an illusion, and we respond by restoring intimacy through Outrageous Acts of Love.

I want to know what love is. What is love? *That* is the next question we ask.

What is love?

And we offer a prayer to take us into the next part of the message—to know what love is.

"I Wanna Know What Love Is" — Foreigner [*See Appendix*]

Every place in the world. Wherever we are coming from. Whether we are in France, or Asia Minor, or Albuquerque, USA. Wherever we are in the world, I want to know what love is. What does that mean?

It means that somehow love has not quite brought us home.

We have listened to all the songs—every song is a love song. We are talking about love; we serve at the altar of love. We often invoke one of the great, sacred moments in contemporary history, a sacred tragic moment: the World Trade Center coming down. It was an epic and tragic scene. People had just a couple of minutes left to do something before their lives ended. They got on their phone, and they called home.

- As much as I love Hebrew wisdom, no one called home and recited the Shema.
- As much as I love Buddhism, no one called home and recited

- the Four Noble Truths.
- As much as I love Christianity, no one called home and recited the Creed.

Everyone called home and everyone said one thing (we have transcripts and they just blow your heart open); everyone called home and said, *I love you.*

You get that?

I love you.

Those three words, that's our sacred creed.

But, what is love?

Ordinary love just doesn't take us home. We have created—all of us together—a new verse, a new sacred verse. The verse is: **We live in a world of outrageous pain. The only response to outrageous pain is Outrageous Love. We live in a world of outrageous beauty, the only response to outrageous beauty is Outrageous Love.**

Let's see if we can just sing it to each other. Then we will go into the next piece of the *dharma*. Then we will move into confession—not confession of sin, but confession of greatness.

Turn to each other. Turn to the person next to you—wherever you are in the world. Turn to yourself. Turn to a person who is not in your room.

This is a chant, an invitation: "How Could Anyone" — Libby Roderick [*See Appendix*]

What do we mean by love? We don't mean ordinary love. We mean Outrageous Love.

We live in a world of outrageous beauty. The only response to outrageous beauty is Outrageous Love. We live in a world of outrageous pain. The only response to outrageous pain is Outrageous Love.

We are not leaving behind.

- We are reclaiming church.
- We are reclaiming prayer.
- We are reclaiming God.

The evolution of Reality is the evolution of God.

The evolution of Reality is the evolution of tears.

The evolution of Reality is the evolution of love.

WHAT DOES LOVE OR OUTRAGEOUS LOVE MEAN AT A HIGHER LEVEL OF CONSCIOUSNESS?

Let's start with the first part of the verse. We live in a world of outrageous pain. What are we saying?

We refuse to dismiss suffering as an illusion.

Every tradition, whether Hindu, Jewish, Buddhist, or Christian has a holy teaching which says:

- It's an illusion.
- If you are just in True Self, you will realize there is no suffering.

And we say to that teaching, *Holy, holy, holy*, and *It only works if you're not suffering*.

It only works if you are not suffering. That is really great to tell that to someone else.

But, when you are suffering, True Self is beautiful. Yes, we need to drop and take refuge in the Buddha. Yes, we need to know we are not merely *Yeish,* say the Kabbalists: I am *Ayin*. I participate in intimate and ultimate consciousness—and any theology that deadens our sensitivity to pain is not kosher.

We have to hold the dignity, look at pain in the eye, and not dismiss it.

THE EVOLUTION OF REALITY IS THE EVOLUTION OF LOVE

We can dismiss it with the old religions or with the New Age. The New Age just reformulates the same idea. In the New Age we say, *if you suffer, you attracted it into your life, and let's tell you exactly how you attracted it into your life.*

The old traditions said, *if you suffer you are being punished.*

We say *Yes* to all the partial truths in that. Deep bow. Thank you, deep bow. Everyone is right. Let's go the next step together.

It is all true—but partial. We have to stand before the Mystery:

- Before the Mystery of a parent passing
- Before the Mystery of a child dying too young
- Before the Mystery of 800,000 people slaughtered in Rwanda

We stand before the Mystery, and we respond to the pain.

We become activists. We hold the dignity of the question. We recognize that the only response to outrageous pain is Outrageous Love.

Because, what is pain? What is suffering? Not the theology; we are not looking for theo-logic. We are past theo-logic. We need to learn how to restore intimacy because what is pain and suffering?

Suffering is a failure of intimacy: *that* is the whole thing.

We are not *romancing* each other.

We are not intimate with each other.

We live in a world of outrageous pain.

When intimacy is true and real, there is no place for outrageous pain. If there's a failure of intimacy, how do we respond? **We respond by restoring intimacy.**

We live in a world of outrageous pain. Let's access the outrageous beauty, which is going to take us back into intimacy. From that outrageous beauty, let's act as Outrageous Lovers and restore intimacy!

Outrageous Love isn't about sexuality—it's got nothing to do with it—bless sexuality, holy, holy, holy—but *that is not what Outrageous Love is about.*

It is not even about romance in the classical sense—you're going to find that one person you are going to romance:

- Outrageous Love is not mere human sentiment.
- Outrageous Love, said Tagore, i*s the heart of existence itself.*
- Dante said, referring to Outrageous Love, it is *the Love that moves the sun and other stars.*
- Charles Peirce wrote, Evolutionary Love is the Eros that drives the whole story, that awakens in me.

We want to awaken and become Outrageous Lovers!

What do we want to do? What is our goal? What is our *kensho*? What is our talking and speaking in tongues? What is our enlightenment? What is the grace that we are looking for? What do Outrageous Lovers do?

- First, Outrageous Lovers keep every boundary that should be kept, of course.
- Of course, they break every boundary of *contraction*—of smallness—that should be broken.

But what do Outrageous Lovers do? Outrageous Lovers commit Outrageous Acts of Love. **That is when we are in our greatness—when we are committing the Outrageous Acts of Love that are ours, and ours alone, to commit.**

If I am great, a Unique Self, an Outrageous Lover, then Reality needs me.

We confess not just our brokenness—we always confess our brokenness and vulnerability—we confess our greatness.

THE EVOLUTION OF REALITY IS THE EVOLUTION OF LOVE

OUR GREATNESS IS IMBUED WITH THE ENORMITY OF THE DESIRE OF EVOLUTION FOR MORE LIFE, MORE LOVE, MORE CREATIVITY

Here is my favorite story about how I learned confessions of greatness. I was walking one day, thanking God for everything. It took a long while. Thanking God for this, thanking God for that, thank you God.

I was then silent having thanked God for everything that I could consider being grateful for.

Then, I heard the words, *Thank you.*

Oh, of course! If I were God, I would be thanking each person for their gifts.

I began to realize that what God was calling for was thanks for my greatness that was given to me, by God. I had to tune into, *what is it?*

It is very hard to tune into your own greatness, but if you know it was given to you by the Higher Power—the universal process of creation—you know it is always going towards more consciousness, freedom, and order.

I'll just say one word about the way I access my greatness: I put it in the Evolutionary Story.

I put myself as an element of the Story, imbued with the enormity of the desire of evolution for more life, more love, more creativity.

Then I see that greatness in me, in *my desire,* for more love, creativity, and giving my gift.

I say, *Thank you God for my greatness*, and I tune into it.

Do you see? Is that possible? Write it in your heart. Let's confess our greatness.

What is my unique greatness?

Confess our greatness, and impress our greatness on the lips of God! And, there is an ecstasy of confession.

In the old church there was an ecstasy of self-abnegation:

> Person 1: I'm a worm.
>
> Person 2: I'm worse than a worm!
>
> Person 1: I'm a nothing.
>
> Person 2: You think *you're* a nothing? *I'm* a nothing.

Right? But we're confessing our greatness,

Om Namah Shivaya.

- We draw from all the traditions.
- We draw from "I Want to Know What Love Is."
- We draw from the great mystic Leonard Cohen's "Hallelujah."
- We draw from "How Could Anyone Ever Tell You."
- We draw from *Om Namah Shivaya.*

Om Namah—we greet. *Shivaya*—the Great Lord Shiva. *Hallelujah.*

BY RE-SOURCING, WE RETURN DEEPER TO OUR SOURCE

This love bypasses all institutions. It's direct. It's our heart to our heart, one to the next. It's the evolution of Evolutionary Love.

It's different from ordinary love.

We are offering to everyone on Earth—all people—the opportunity to express evolutionary love because that impulse lives inside everyone.

We cultivate that impulse; we have faith in that impulse.

It's easy to lose faith in your own impulse.

Everyone loses faith in their own impulse at some point!

THE EVOLUTION OF REALITY IS THE EVOLUTION OF LOVE

But it's all there.

Let us join together to give the resources to re-source humanity.

The person who is giving to this particular activity is returning deeper to their source.

CHAPTER NINE

INTERCONNECTION, INTIMACY, AND A MEMORY OF THE FUTURE

Episode 19 — March 4, 2017

HEALING SEPARATION

Our theme is that global action comes from shared intimacy. How do we even imagine intimacy on a global scale, dealing with the suffering of our world?

Take some deep breaths.

Breathe into the feeling in yourself of wherever there is a pain in the world that you can recognize.

Feel yourself somewhere, anywhere in the world, the children, the people in the camps, the people in the wars, the people dying, the people sick, the people fighting—anywhere.

Now go within to the Unique Self within you, pulsing with the experience of the billions of years of evolution in you, pulsing toward giving your gift somewhere in the world. Now look at where that pain is taking you.

What part of the pain of the world is your Unique Self drawn to?

Let your attention go there just spontaneously, wherever it most uniquely goes, to whatever pain it most uniquely experiences. Feel that universal self—that Unique Self encoded with the Evolutionary Love of the Universe itself—going to that pain. Send it there.

How does it feel when your uniqueness enters into the feeling of pain somewhere in the world?

My Unique Self is going to all those whose Unique Self is hidden from them and who feel lost. Where is your Unique Self going, into what pain?

We are going to experience the healing from the intimacy of Unique Self touching another at the very source of the pain which in a deep sense is almost always separation. We are healing the separation, connecting our Unique Self, wherever that pain may be in the world.

IN THE INTIMATE UNIVERSE, NO ONE IS LEFT OUT OF THE CIRCLE

We are about feeling each other. **Our entire vision is a vision of what we call an Intimate Universe.** We are laying down the deep structures of the new creed which is the realization that:

- We are God's deed.
- We live in an Intimate Universe.
- Intimacy is the nature of Reality itself.

Just feel that sutra, that verse, that epigram, that deep realization, as we enter into the field of resonant prayer—**we live in an Intimate Universe!**

To be able to feel means to feel someone else's pain and also someone else's joy.

I'll tell you a little holy secret as we move into prayer. They say that there are three kinds of friends.

- One kind of friend is just a good friend and goes along with you in life. They can really empathize with you.
- There is a higher kind of friend. When you're in pain, a higher kind of friend—that very unique, rare friend—can be with you in the pain and feel your pain.
- There is an even higher friend which is the highest of the high, the Holy of Holies, the deepest of the deep. That is a friend who can be with you when you are up, when you are ecstatic, when you are so excited, and that friend can feel your joy.

We are entering together into the truth of Reality. We live in an Intimate Universe: No one's alone, no one's separate, and no one's cut off.

As we enter into this twenty-first century, we realize for the first time, *we are all interconnected*. I want to say it, just this huge sentence. If you really get it, it will blow your heart wide open. Fritjof Capra did such a great job in 1996 in popularizing Systems Science. Ken Wilber did a great job, also in 1996, putting out a book called *Sex, Ecology, Spirituality* which was also about the deep sense of Systems Science.

> ## *Systems Science says that we are all interconnected.*

It's all connected. What Capra was talking about was interconnectivity, and **interconnectivity is the outside of it**. It's the exterior—the realization in chaos theory, complexity theory, that we are all interconnected.

But intimacy—and this is the sentence that will just blow your heart open if you really get it—is the interior of interconnectivity. The way interconnectivity feels on the inside is intimate.

The inside of interconnectivity is intimacy, that's the Dharma. That is the essence: the realization that not only are we interconnected, as evolutionary science reminds us, but as interior enlightenment science reminds us, **we are intimate.**

GOD OF INTIMACY

As we move into prayer now, what are we saying? Prayer says one thing. It's not about praying to a puppeteer God who moves us around demanding blind obedience and punishing us if we masturbate. That's not what it's about—**it's so much deeper.**

The Evolutionary God is the God of intimacy because evolution is the evolution of intimacy, and we live in an Intimate Universe.

Prayer affirms the intimacy of Reality. Prayer is the realization that God is not merely the Infinity of Power, God is the Infinity of Intimacy.

It's all intimate. It's all not just interconnected; it is all in contact. We are affecting each other. We need each other. The source of all that intimacy is none other than what Ramakrishna would call *Mother!* The source of all intimacy, the Infinity of Intimacy that knows our name, and everything we experience. If you might have had a hard moment yesterday morning, let's say at 8:30, and you cried for a moment, at that moment *the Infinity of Intimacy, Mother, held and drank all those tears.*

Every time we cry, God drinks in our tears, and every time we laugh, God laughs with us.

We may live, occasionally, lives of quiet desperation, but there are never lives of *lonely* desperation. So, we turn to God and bring before the altar of the Infinity of Intimacy, the altar of God. We bring before God everything. We bring before God our *holy and our broken Hallelujah,* and with this, we pray.

Amen.

It's a holy and a broken Hallelujah. We bring it all: every tear, every piece of laughter. We begin to offer our prayer, and we pray for everything.

> *What do we ask for when we pray? We ask for everything because prayer affirms the dignity of personal need.*

No one's left out of the circle. We are whole mates, we are rocking it open in the world, together. We are making mistakes, and we're making mistakes in the right direction. We pray that we can all make mistakes in the right direction and we can come together.

Let these teachings not be a mask for ego. Let planetary missions not be a mask for our emptiness but let it come from our fullness, from our goodness. There's room for everyone, no one's left out of the circle.

Let us, together, play a larger game and participate in the Evolution of Love. We lay the groundwork for a new world order, as we begin to heal the global intimacy disorder and begin to act as love.

THIS EXTRAORDINARY MOMENT IN HISTORY

The evolutionary impulse rides through us like a hurricane. It rides through us like a flood of love; it's really true.

The French use a riddle to teach schoolchildren the nature of exponential growth. A lily pond, so the riddle goes, contains a single leaf. Each day, the number of leaves doubles, two leaves the second day, four the third, eight the fourth and so on. If the pond is full on the 30th day, at what point is it half-full? Answer, on the 29th day.

In other words, it took this long in the entire history of planet Earth—from its origin billions of years ago as a rock, when on came the first life forms, and then built the biosphere and emerged all the species, and then came

INTERCONNECTION, INTIMACY, AND A MEMORY OF THE FUTURE

Homo sapiens, the self-conscious species—and now we, the self-conscious species, are being told that:

- our very greatness,
- our ability to reproduce, to populate, to create,
- our ability to span the world with internet,
- our ability to reach out like gods,
- our entire creative capability to sustain life…

…has brought us to the almost last day of life on earth.

This is a *huge* shock to a creative species.

When I (Barbara) graduated from college in 1951, I was told all the problems had been solved. So this last day, before the population and the pollution go exponential—we are born on that last day. All of us have arisen on the last day.

THE LAST DAY OF THE CREATION OF THE OLD IS OBVIOUSLY THE FIRST DAY OF THE CREATION OF THE NEW

Take a moment to imagine the pain, the shock, and the reality that if this generation does not respond, it will be very difficult for life to be sustained—human life as we know it will disappear.

This means that, for the very first time, on the next to the last day of this stage of creation, the Unique Self in every one of us—which is on the interior of evolution—has woken up en masse. **The inner impulse, the Unique Self, particularly the Evolutionary Unique Self, is the impulse of evolution incarnate in every one of us on the next to the last day of the old phase of evolution.**

Is that true?

It is true.

Go within and feel the Unique Self, the impulse of evolution recognizing that we declare that every day is irreducibly unique, every day has a Unique Self, and every day has a unique gift that comes from the newness that comes from the evolutionary impulse. Each one of us can feel the unique impulse of evolution available each day.

The last day of the old age is precisely honored as the first day of the new creation.

Millions of us are shifting rapidly right now, into the awareness that we are connected, we are whole, and we are expressions of the entire process of creation.

Tune into your own Unique Self and, if you can, your Evolutionary Unique Self—the one that is impelled by this entire process of creation. Tune into where it most yearns to go to express its love. Where does your Unique Self yearn to go?

This is not just, *Oh it's such a challenge, it's so terribly difficult to help and to deal with this crisis.*

It's just the opposite.

This is where you can feel the most love. This is the exact crisis or pain or hurt or need that YOU are designed to express love for.

Go in and see if there's a specific expression of your Unique Self, of love, where it's most needed—how it feels to you when you express where it's needed. Imagine the peak experience (that is to say you're at your best when doing this), wherever your Unique Self is most yearning to go to connect, to create your peak experience.

It's very specific.

Mine is communication—I feel peak experience and am now imagining a planetary awakening. I imagine Marc, myself, and all of us, our voices being heard on a planetary scale, in our nervous system, leading to the Planetary Awakening in Love. I am feeling that now.

Please turn within and find a *specific* expression that you are doing; it has to be really specific for it to be a peak experience.

How does it feel to you when you do it? How does it feel when you're actually on target with where your Unique Self means to go? Your Unique Self longs to go there. Whoo!

Let's imagine stimulating a planetary symphony, a Unique Self Symphony of everybody on Earth who wants to give their gift, uniquely, into the planetary nervous system to turn us on to the first day of the second creation.

That is the actual possibility.

That is the realistic intention.

That is the holy opportunity we are given in the Evolutionary Church.

I ask that we intend to be the catalytic agent, the sourcing code of love and creativity, directed to awakening humanity collectively. Thank you God.

FROM ATONEMENT TO ATTUNEMENT

Imagine, imagine the disciples walking in Bethlehem. Imagine when the new order was formed around the great teachings of Buddha.

We're all the Buddha together.

The Evolutionary Church is the Buddha. The Buddha's not Marc, and the Buddha's not Barbara, although Barbara does begin with a B. But that's not how it works. The next Buddha is the *sangha*; it is the Unique Self Symphony.

We are a symphony of stars.

Why do we call it a Unique Self Symphony? Because **everyone plays their unique instrument, and that unique instrument is in deep resonance** with the entire symphony. Without that particular instrument, the entire symphony is not attuned.

We have gotten so good, in religion and spirituality, at atonement. Maybe we need to get better at attunement. From atonement to attunement. We attune to the evolutionary impulse awakening in us.

> *Who are we? We are messengers who forgot our message.*

When we recover our message, then the message is impressed on the lips of God who lives in us and as us and yet who holds us.

Let's not use the word *you* at all. It's not, *you're joining us*. There's no you, there's no us.

We are the Buddha, together.

WE ARE THE UNIQUE SELF SYMPHONY: LET'S FEEL IT ARISE

I'm going to tell you a story about Nachman of Breslov. It's a story about Unique Self Symphony. It's a story about how we know that **uniqueness is the currency of connection**, which is one of our core verses.

- Verse one: We live in an Intimate Universe
- Verse two: Uniqueness is the currency of connection.

How do you connect in the Intimate Universe?

You connect not by making yourself like everyone else but by being the unique instrument that you are in the symphony. Your uniqueness is not your separateness—separateness separates, uniqueness connects. That's the core teaching dharma of Unique Self—**uniqueness is the currency of connection.**

When Barbara is in her Barbara-ness, do we connect to her?

She blows our minds. To the precise extent that Barbara's not quite being Barbara, we can't feel her. To the precise extent that Marc's not quite being Marc, we can't feel him. But the most authentic, unique Barbara—she doesn't separate from us—she blows our minds and our hearts wide open. Great poetry, great Irish poetry, is not when the Irish are trying to be Swedish. It's when you're so Irish, **so in your irreducible uniqueness, it just blows the heart over the whole thing.**

THE INSANE KING

I want to tell you a story from the mystical tradition. It's a story that Franz Kafka loved. It's a story about where we are today in the United States.

But this is not an American church:

- It's a Mexican church,
- It's a German church.
- It's an African church.
- It's an Asian church.
- It's a Chinese church.

We become Unique Self Symphony.

So, here's the story.

It's a story about a king who has a very close friend. They are super close, and they love each other so much. One day, they realized (and remember Kafka loved this story for a reason) that the grain had been poisoned. When you eat the grain, you don't die; you just go insane. You don't know what's true—fake news, alternative facts. What's going on? You can't figure out what's actually happening.

All the people are eating the grain, and they're going insane. If there's *no ground*, as the great poet Yeats said, *the center doesn't hold.*

Wow, *The center doesn't hold*. We become the *hollow men*, the *stuffed men*. The center is not holding. Wow!

But they're not sure, the king and counsel to the king of this great kingdom. What should we do? Should we eat the grain and go insane with them, or because we're the king and the counselor, should we separate ourselves from them so at least we'll be sane, and we'll be able to rule the kingdom?

They're not sure.

Finally, the king says, *You know what? I can't be separated from my kingdom. Everyone's going insane. I'm going to go insane with them.*

The counselor says, I *understand, my good friend the king, but let's at least make a mark on our foreheads. We'll make a mark on our foreheads, and we'll look at each other say, "What's that mark?" and we'll remember. We'll remember our sanity. We'll remember that we're insane.*

What a crazy, holy story. You see, friends, it's okay when we've forgotten. It's okay to forget, but when we've forgotten that we've forgotten, oh my god, then we have to find our way back. Each of us, we have a mark on our foreheads. The mark on our foreheads is not to remember. It can't take us that far; it is to remember that we have forgotten.

Remember that we've forgotten. **We have not just forgotten a memory of our past; we have forgotten the memory of our future.**

HOPE IS A MEMORY OF THE FUTURE

Verse three: Hope is a memory of the future.

We are writing a Great Library that articulates the memory of the future. We are calling for a Planetary Awakening through Unique Self Symphony that awakens a memory of the future. We are committed—all of us—to *articulating* the memory of that future.

If you think there's someone else to do it, you are profoundly mistaken.

Only you can do it.

The mark on your forehead is your Unique Self.

- It is *your* unique allurement.
- It is the unique gift that only *you* can give
- It is *your* Evolutionary Unique Self.

You feel the impulse of evolution awakening uniquely in you, as you, and through you, and you're allured in a way that no one else is.

You realize you have a gift to give, and that gift can be given by the Outrageous Love that's you, by no one that ever was, is, or will be. Your Unique Self is the mark on your forehead, and the *dharma* is the mark on the collective forehead of culture as we awaken as love. We can't just awaken as love. We have to pray, to actually know what love truly is.

Love is Outrageous Love.

There is no greater goal than everyone waking up in the morning, and they say, *I am an irreducibly, gorgeous Unique Self. I am an irreducibly unique expression of the LoveIntelligence, and we live in an Intimate Universe.*

As we've said—this Evolutionary Church, this evolutionary synagogue, this evolutionary mosque, this evolutionary zendo, this evolutionary, secular, humanist place of gathering—we feel each other.

We've got to correct the old mistake of evolutionary spirituality, which charges the barricades to change the world but forgets about the irreducible gorgeousness of the person right next to me.

We live in an Intimate Universe.

What does it mean to live in an Intimate Universe?

To live in an Intimate Universe is to live in intimacy. Intimacy means:

- I am *aligned* with the evolutionary impulse that lives in me.

- I am *in touch* with the unique allurements that connect me to the larger field.
- *I don't bypass anything*, I can feel myself.

The first step of intimacy, my friends is to feel myself. To feel myself is to feel my Unique Self, my unique allurements.

The second step of intimacy is to feel you. To feel you is to shift my perspective and feel you, your pain, your joy, and your unique allurements.

And then I go even a step higher: I feel you feeling me. I feel you feeling me, and you feel me, feeling you.

And I go a step even higher, and **actually the circle goes around once again.**

I feel you feeling me, feeling you.

Do you begin to see how it works? It goes deeper and deeper between us. That's the first way **we deepen intimacy. Then, we expand intimacy.**

I feel not only you but the person next to you.

I feel not only the survival of my people but my whole tribe.

Then I begin to feel the whole world, and I feel the whole Cosmos.

But so often what we do, my beloved friends, is: We go to feel the Cosmos, and we skip the person next to us.

So, we've got to bring it all in. **We've got to transcend and include until we can feel the whole thing, and the Intimate Universe explodes as us.** We turn to the whole world when we sing for the last time. We finish with this deep knowing, this deep chant: *om nama shivaya*.

And as the Hindus do, we greet Lord Shiva, who lives in all of us.

Om Namah Shivaya

Om Namah Shivaya
Shivaya namaha,
Shivaya namah om
Shivaya namaha, namaha Shivaya
Shambhu Shankara namah Shivaya,
Girijaa Shankara namah Shivaya
Arunaachala Shiva namah Shivaya

I bow to the Soul of all. I bow to my Self. I don't know who I am, so I bow to you, Shiva, my own true Self. I bow to my teachers who loved me with Love. Who took care of me when I couldn't take care of myself. I owe everything to them. How can I repay them? They have everything in the world. Only my love is mine to give, but in giving, I find that it is their love flowing through me back to the world…I have nothing. I have everything. I want nothing. Only let it flow to you, my love… sing!

The holy *sangha*.

It's all of us, together.

We are the Unique Self Symphony, friends.

It does not get better than this.

CHAPTER TEN

BECOMING AGENTS OF INTIMACY FOR A NEW STORY

Episode 20 — March 11, 2017

INNOVATION ON THE INSIDE: YOU BECOME THE AGENT OF INTIMACY

We are dedicated to the awakening of humanity, to connecting us with Source worldwide—a *mighty* mission. I would like to take us through a passageway to this sense of union.

I start with loneliness. Underneath the intimacy, every one of us, at some point in life, feels profound loneliness.

Tune into how it feels when you are not connected at all. When I feel that, I almost feel as though I am dying. From that profound experience of separation and loneliness, go deeper and see if you can touch into the source of creation, God, the impulse within you.

Out of the loneliness, go deep down into Source and invite it, breathe it up, in through the loneliness. Feel that God Source you are breathing up, uniquely expressing itself as you.

Where does the loneliness go?

As that God Source is expressing uniquely as you, feel your expression reaching out to anyone else you might have felt separated from. Then, breathe into the Source of creation within that person. Breathe it up the whole way through them, feeling the God impulse coming up through a separated self, as it is coming up through you.

What happens when you align the unique impulse of the God Self in yourself with the other that you feel separated from? Do a simultaneous breath with the two of you.

I am smiling because it is not possible for me to be totally separated from the God Self arising up in you, and me, and the person that you could not get along with. In fact, it's funny!

Feel that vibrational field coming up through you and coming up through someone you have felt separated from. Now, expand it out into your family, everybody that you know nearby, each unique, each vibrating, each coming from the same Source, each somewhat alone but joined through you.

You become the agent of intimacy. Wow!

LONELINESS ON TWO LEVELS

Loneliness is an incentive because it cannot be resolved other than through this. Imagine that everybody has reached out further to those they know. Feel the Unique Self Symphony. Is there anybody on Earth that does not have a vibrational field of that? Is there anybody who would not like to feel it resonating beyond themselves in the *Infinity of Intimacy*?

Loneliness is an experience on two levels.

On one level, loneliness is this personal feeling of not being received. You have so much you want to share, and you want to transmit the essence of who you are. You want to share your *soul print*. The soul print is like the fingerprint. It is the DNA of who you are. To be lonely is to be unable to share your soul print with another person.

That is level one loneliness.

But even when you can share your soul print with another person, even when you can share your life, your stuff, your fears, and your early childhood, even when you can share your wounds and bind it in the whole story, you can still be lonely, even after you do the entire thing—*oh my mother never took care of me! It's all her fault!*

Yes, we do need to share with each other!

On a second level, we are deeper beings than just the psychology of our woundedness. We are drawn forward by the lure of becoming. We are drawn forward by the evolutionary impulse that lives in us.

We remain lonely if we cannot share the evolutionary impulse, our yearning, or our greatness. If we cannot share how we show up—not just as a fingerprint or soul print but as unique expressions of the entire evolutionary process, as *LoveIntelligence* come alive in us, as us, and through us, we remain lonely:

> *We have to share not just our brokenness but also our greatness as an evolutionary impulse.*

EXISTENTIAL RISK

I had deep conversations with some people who are very, very close to me. This is when I said, *I'm really scared.* We talked about existential risk, about the danger to the planet, about just being scared out of our minds because this is not like from time immemorial when there were threats of catastrophe and Armageddon. Those were mythic threats; those were metaphors.

For the first time, we are challenged by a level of power that can *actually* destroy us!

Whatever Attila the Hun could do, he did not have the capacity to destroy the world. We have seven or eight major existential threats that could destroy the world.

At the Center for Integral Wisdom, our think-tank, our action-tank, our love-tank, we are trying to articulate a new vision, a new code, that carries us forward—alive. One of our textbooks is *The Infinite Resource*, by Ramez Naam, where he lays out the eight or nine major existential risks. We are at the edge of Armageddon. It is true. We could blow ourselves up in about eight or nine different ways.

Recently, someone who is very close to me said:

> I do not know what to do about this. Do I take this in? I do not feel motivated by it. I am not motivated by the fact that it could all blow up. On the other hand, it has been that way forever. Is there anything new in this? What can I do about it? I just shut it out because what else can I do with that information?

IN THE FACE OF EXISTENTIAL RISK, WE DO NOT HAVE TO DO THE WHOLE THING

Let's go really slow for a second. The truth is, there is a real risk that never existed before, which is our new level of power. Ramez Naam lays out in his book, *The Infinite Resource*, the eight or nine major risks, but then Ramez Naam becomes hopeful.

Why is he hopeful? He is hopeful because there is innovation because we can innovate. *Innovation*—connecting co-creators worldwide with what is working. Like our Wheel of Co-Creation 2.0. But Ramez Naam's great weakness in his book, and the great weakness of Peter Diamandis and the whole gang, including Ray Kurzweil, is: They talk about innovation only on an exterior level—technological innovation of all sorts, from nanotechnology to new kinds of microchips to space travel. They all talk about exterior innovation, space travel, and Elon Musk. And thank you, Elon Musk, holy man! Get us into space, yes!

What we are saying, with the Center for Integral Wisdom, the Foundation for Conscious Evolution, and Evolutionary Church, what we're all saying together is that innovation on the outside will not change the game. Exterior innovation by itself will not shift the story. We will blow ourselves up, and we are going to do it much sooner than later.

The risk is real!

> *What we need is also innovation on the inside.*

The Renaissance was *interior innovation*. The Renaissance introduced:

- A new vision
- A new Universe Story
- A new vision of man and woman
- A new vision of relationship
- A new vision of what is possible

It wasn't technology. It was *new interior technology*. It was a new story.

A NEW UNIVERSE STORY RAISES ALL BOATS

Did you know that at the time of the Renaissance everyone in the world had slaves? There was no one anywhere in the world who was not a slave owner. The world was filled with slavery.

Within 100 years of the new vision of interiors, the new vision of human rights, the new vision of human dignity, which was based on a new Universe

Story, for the first time in history—slavery was abolished in every place in the world.

That is new technology!

What we are doing together is introducing a new set of memetic structures, new memes:

- A new Universe Story
- A new story of Unique Self and Unique Self Symphony
- New levels of evolutionary relationships
- A new vision of pleasure as the source of ethics
- A new vision of a Telerotic Universe

I want to be vulnerable here. What we are trying to do, in loving each other, is bring our memes together.

That is sexy! **Only a new Renaissance, a new Western enlightenment, a new Universe Story, is going to change the game. Together, we are bringing:**

- Conscious Evolution,
- Unique Self Symphony, and
- Planetary Awakening with the evolution of the source code…

…in order to create a telerotic world event, which is the introduction of a new Universe Story.

That is what we are doing.

It is not like, *hey, can we make everyone feel good with another New Age event, have a nice time*—fuck that! Pardon the expression. I apologize. Sorry, I take that back. But, this is not a cute thing; *let's hang out and have a good time.*

The world is in danger! It is actually true! There is genuine existential risk.

The good news is:

- We can do something about it.
- We have to take it in.
- We have to be willing to take the existential risk into our hearts.

We take it in, not to paralyze us because it is hard, but to inspire us because we do not have to do the whole thing. We are Unique Selves, with unique Outrageous Acts of Love to commit that no one else can.

You see, when you say your heart constricts and closes, that is only when you think you have to do the whole thing. You do not have to do the whole thing. You need to play your role and your instrument in the Unique Self Symphony. You can respond to the unique need by giving your unique gift!

Let us stop creating global movements that exist only in Colorado, in Portland, Oregon, and in San Francisco. A global movement of the same 200,000 people talking to each other, all living on the Western Seaboard of the United States, and we call it a global movement—are we for real!? Let's create an Evolutionary Church with millions of people listening in China, India, and Asia.

No, we have got to create a truly global movement, and imagine a world in which everybody is bringing their *holy and broken Halleluja*h to church. We are articulating these memes, and we are spreading this in the world, and we have the technology to do it! Wow!

WE HEAR GOD IN THE DEEP, SMALL VOICE

In every generation, there's a small group of people who say:

> We are going to take that existential risk in. We are not going to run away from it. We are going to respond. We are going to give it all we have, not just cutely, not just in a little seminar. We are going to change our lives and be unique selves and step up and build the Center for Integral Wisdom, build a Foundation for Conscious Evolution, build a planetary mission, and build an

Evolutionary Church. It is all the same thing.

Let it spread into the world! Let bells of liberation ring throughout the land. We bring our holy and our broken *Hallelujah*. Thank you so much. Amen.

I pray for my mother. I pray for all of us to be our unique selves. I pray that I wake up as an extraordinary lover every day!

We can be gentle and quiet. We can live in the pair of dice. We are going to lead into the *holy and broken Halleluja*h of our prayer. Prayer affirms the dignity of personal need; we don't bypass woundedness. Our prayers are offered. Our prayers are received. All obstacles are melted away. The word is good.

God lives in the still, small voice. Yes, we can be gentle and quiet.

- God is not only quiet.
- Spirit is not only quiet.
- Spirit is *being*, which is deep solitude, deep, gorgeous quiet.
- Spirit is also *becoming*.
- It is ecstatically urgent.
- It is tumultuous.
- It is alive.
- It is ecstatic.
- It is Evangelical.
- It's bringing the good news.

Somehow, the New Age has become all about silence. Evangelicals became all about crying out, *Hallelujah*! **We have to hold both.**

We have to bring them both together. We hear God in the deep, small voice. We hear God in the ecstatic urgency of the good news that we can bring the new story. That new story can raise all boats and transform everything. Barbara, bring us the still, small voice. Bring us the ecstatic urgency. Bring us the new story, Beloved.

JOINING GENIUS ON A META SCALE

I'm here now speaking on the very great theme of, *how would this work?* This is the feminine co-creator stepping up into the masculine *Hallelujah*. We give birth to babies. Our bodies do the most amazing miracles, and when that baby comes out, it's radically new and radically precious, every single one of them.

My theme today is *social synergy*. I would like to say a word about social synergy, and by believing in it, we can do it.

For billions and billions of years, the impulse of evolution has had this extraordinary power. When things are not working well, like in the five mass extinctions that came before us, these things happened:

- Innovations
- Creative solutions
- More love

Nature has designed it so those innovations connect with each other and create radical newness out of the chaos. You begin to notice, if you look at the billions of years of evolution, that nature uses dysfunctionality, disintegration, and chaos as the raw materials for emergence, creativity, and more.

What does that make us feel about the Armageddon threat that we are now facing? It's real, and it has to be real, now. This is what an evolutionary feels. Nature is giving us the opportunity to join genius on a meta scale. We are lucky enough to think of joining genius with one other person, but imagine for the moment, nature is in us. Every single person has an innate impulse of the creation of genius. Everyone.

We are all facing the same crisis. This is another really good thing about it. It's not a crisis to the east of the world, the west of the world, only for the Christians of the world, or the Jews of the world. No.

It is a global crisis.

Nature has done a really good job on this one because:

- It seems to be climate change,
- It seems to be the loss of our oceans,
- It seems to be the running out of the proper air for people to breathe,
- It seems to be New York is going to go 12 feet under,
- It seems like everyone is going to be dislodged.

Good job, evolution!

I'm saying this because I'm going to be dislodged myself. I already am, and it's painful. However, if you're one of the people on Earth who knows this crisis and it pains you, whether it means you have to migrate from your island, leave New York, or create a whole new lover, you recognize that nature is with you if you can join with others.

The way these innovations out of the dysfunctional system work is that they tend to connect with each other. At a certain point, they go into quantum, non-local, exponential interaction. When I read that in 1977, I said, *well, why don't we try it*—that is to say, we humans. *If nature has been doing it for billions of years, let us try it!*

WHEN SYNCON SECTORS BECAME CONNECTED, IT WAS A SOCIAL LOVE AFFAIR

I invented something called *Syncon*, which stands for "synergistic convergence." This is very literal. How do you synergize? It is not easy, but here is how you do it:

We built huge wheels in large university auditoriums, and we created the sectors: health, education, economics, science, and technology. We invited people to go into those sectors, almost all of whom did not agree with each other. We invited environmentalists, and next to them, we put business people who want to build, where the environmentalists want to save it. We brought welfare mothers. We brought very wealthy people. We brought *whites and blacks*. We made an experiment with my partner, John Whiteside, an Air Force colonel. Here is what we did:

We said: *each group come in, into the center of the wheel*. We had little TV cameras, and people walked into a new structure. This is a key to social synergy on a political level—you cannot do it in rows. John Whiteside said, *If somebody stands up and talks to six people in rows, they will not do it.*

We form a circle with all these sectors—environment, business, health, etc. Every sector says what they need. They say in an assembly of the whole, *this is what we need that we do not have.*

Here is synergy. I say to all of you: *This is what I really need to create what I know I need for the Evolutionary Church. Is there anybody who has a resource to meet my need?*

This is what we did in the big circle: *Is there anybody who has a resource?* If I'm an environmentalist and I'm next to the business group or next to the government group, what happened was somebody from business had a resource to meet the need of the environmentalist, who could not do it without the government.

The government said, *I could communicate that if you would let me know what you are doing.* Then, the media came in, and before you knew, it every single sector that was in isolation when trying to vote became connected when they tried to create.

At the very end, we had assemblies of the whole with all these opposing groups, each of which had been given more of what they needed by the others.

It was a huge love affair. It was a social love affair.

The result of social synergy is social love.

BECOMING AGENTS OF INTIMACY FOR A NEW STORY

The truth of the matter is nobody can fully get what they want to create without joining genius with others, just as nobody can create a baby without there being *sperm and egg* connecting. Nobody can fully get what they want if they're not going to find the others, whose location meets their needs and vice versa.

I believe we tapped into the beginning of synergistic democracy with twenty-five huge conferences, including gang leaders of Los Angeles who were burning the city down. It did not matter when we brought the gang leaders. We brought Gene Roddenberry and Ray Bradbury. We mixed the people. The gang leaders had to talk to policemen, the welfare mothers they'd hurt, and a great science fiction writer who completely blew their minds. We mixed the people, and they all talked face-to-face about what they wanted to create.

I would like to say we do some huge and wonderful events of social synergy. We bring our idea of the politics of love and the vast creativity of celebration to this social synergy event I am imagining. We are going to celebrate greatness. We are going to join our greatness with each other's greatness. We are going to *be* it with each other.

I am going to say that the reason Donald Trump and Hillary Clinton could not do it is because they did not understand social synergy.

Liberal democracy, which was great at the time of monarchy, has gotten itself stuck everywhere in the world.

- It's not working in Europe.
- It's not working in South America.
- It's not working in Mexico.

Why not?

It is the wrong structure. We declare it has to be a wheel. We are reinventing the wheel. At the heart of the wheel is Spirit and everybody's passion, uniquely as them, joined.

We will initiate social synergy.

We will discover what it means at a time when democracy is failing and when Armageddon is threatening. **We are inspired by the Spirit of evolution towards a planetary awakening in a Unique Self Symphony.**

This is the right goal—this is what to do! If anybody comes up to you and says, *I don't know what to do; I'm scared of Armageddon,* You say, *here's what to do. We are going to create social synergy*—they will not know what it is—*we are going to have a blessed Hallelujah, of connecting humanity to co-create before it is too late.*

REALITY IS A STORY, AND IT'S GOING SOMEWHERE

We are going to emerge, to synergize together at this higher level of resonance. We are doing it for two reasons: one is that it's going to make us happy, which is our real goal in life, and two is, we have to heal.

It's *all* one.

As a thought experiment, I am going to introduce a friend of mine. His name is Steve Bannon. I like Steve. He got a new job at the White House, which is cool, with my Ortho-Jewish friend Jared Kushner and Ivanka—hanging out at the White House. Steve is a cool guy. We demonize Steve a lot, but he is an interesting dude. He says some interesting things. He has about half of it right; he has half of it wrong. When we demonize a person, we stop the conversation. That is a demon; let's not talk to demons. Actually, let's stop demonizing because Steve Bannon is not demonic. He is just half-right, and his half-right is really important. What he gets wrong is important, also. So, Steve, this is for you man, with a lot of love, a lot of respect, a lot of honor. Listen up, I would love to hear your response.

Steve loves this book, *The Fourth Turning: An American Prophecy*, by William Strauss and Neil Howe, which talks about these 80-year cycles of history. When this book first came out in 1997, Al Gore liked the book so much that he gave it to every member of Congress. It's a good book. What it says is that every 80 years things shift. The 80 years are split into four 20-year cycles called *saeculum*. Everything unfolds in these 20-year turnings.

The first turning is a season of rebirth, social unity, and building new institutions. Let us say in our American generational cycle, the first turning is the post-World War II period.

That is followed by a second turning characterized by a spiritual awakening, a rejection of the previous turning of values. The values of the 1950s are insufficient, and there is this explosion of new Spirit. That is the 1960s, rock and roll, and feminism.

Then, we get to a third turning in the 1980s: greed starts to unravel. We start to lose faith in institutions; we lose faith in business as usual. The explosion of Spirit in the second turning did not bring us home. We lose faith.

Then, the fourth turning, which probably began with the financial crisis of 2008. It is a breakdown, where social institutions collapse, and the way is clear for the next first turning, and the 80-year cycle starts again.

Barbara, you love this story. It is the story of the butterfly. It is the famous story of the worm that becomes a butterfly. The way it happens structurally is when the worm eats for 300 days, it hangs itself on a hook, completely bloated, and then completely dissolves. Within that dissolving, an earlier genome structure exists in the worm. Scientists were completely baffled by this—that in one genome structure, there is already an implicit new genome structure. These imaginal cells come together and form the butterfly.

That famous image is always about the fourth turning, when the social institutions break down in order to make room for a new first turning. That is what Steve Bannon basically believes, and he's right. We are at a fourth turning. Our institutions are failing.

What Steve Bannon fails to understand—and Steve, my friend, this is for you, with total love—what you're missing, holy brother, is the way you tell the story. It is like Mircea Eliade's *Myth of the Eternal Return*; it keeps going round and round again. It never gets anywhere. That is the tragedy of the way you tell the story.

In your vision, and in Strauss and Howe's vision, when the fourth turning breaks down, we start again. We go through all four again. It is a circle, and it goes round and round and round.

Like Harry Chapin singing *All My Life's A Circle*: (Marc *singing*) *all my life's a circle / sunrise and sundown / the moon moves through the mountain*. Harry Chapin used to sing this. We would listen to it in a factory when I was 15 that I worked at in Columbus, Ohio. I came back 40 years later; everyone was listening to Harry Chapin sing, *All My Life's A Circle*. The same people, in the same warehouse. No one had moved. It had not transformed.

We do not need a circle. We need a spiral.

The evolutionary people say it is all moving forward with this great liberal progress. That is nonsense!

That is why Trump won the election—because the liberal world is insular, self-congratulatory, and lives in its upper-middle-class bubble, congratulating itself, taking one workshop after the other. Yet…

- We forget about all the men losing manufacturing jobs in Middle America.
- We forget about the crisis.
- We want to deny existential risk.
- We want to go to our little retreats and have our little transformations.
- We do not take in the tragedy and suffering of the world.

The line of evolutionary progress is a lie.

But the circle of it, going round and round again, is the old Hindu image, which Strauss and Howe picked up, that drives my friend Steve Bannon—that is a lie also.

There is a profound spiral. We are spiraling up. Reality is not a fact, it is a Story, and it is going somewhere. It gets higher each time.

My friend, Steve, holy brother—it;s driven by Evolutionary Eros. It's not an accidental chance story. It's not random.

> Read *The Systems View of Life: A Unifying Vision,* by Fritjof Capra and Pier Luigi Luisi
>
> Read *Reinventing the Sacred: A New View of Science, Reason and Religion,* by Stuart Kauffman
>
> Read *The Self-Organizing Universe,* by Erich Jantsch

Add them, my brother Steve Bannon, to your reading of *The Fourth Turning: An American Prophecy* by William Strauss and Neil Howe.

You will begin to realize this story is going somewhere. It is driven by Evolutionary Love. With each turning of the wheel, we introduce new structures.

- We have the potential to up-level, to create heaven on Earth.
- We can do it better than it was ever done before.
- We are making progress.
- We are moving forward.
- We are participating in the evolution of love.
- We are able to play a larger game.

Once you get that, my brother Steve, something new comes into your heart.

What comes into your heart that's new is hope. Hope! Hope is a memory of the future. We are articulating a memory of the future. We are called forth by that memory of the future. That memory of the future is not just a recycling of eternal myths of the return of yesterday. We have the potential to become something different than we have ever been.

HOPE IS A MEMORY OF THE FUTURE

What is true is that it always breaks down before it gets better.

We have got to be willing to endure the breakdown in order to have the breakthrough.

- It breaks down with crisis.
- It breaks down when we get attacked and demonized.
- It breaks down when things in our lives happen in ways that we cannot imagine would happen that way.
- We need to be able to enter into the deep and gorgeous brokenness in order to become whole.

This is why we chose Leonard Cohen's song. Because he says that all of it *is* drawn from our lips, *the holy and the broken Hallelujah*. There is nothing more whole than a broken heart.

Tragically, I have talked to so many New Age people, so many human potential people. They are willing to throw their integrity out and throw their truth out because they say:

- We have to move forward with our programs!
- We have to save the world!
- We have to do our stuff!
- We have to lie a little bit!
- We have to give up our integrity!
- We have to throw a few people overboard!
- It does not matter!
- It is for the sake of the story!

No! We do not give up truth for the sake of this new goodness.

Goodness, truth, and beauty live together.

You cannot give up the good.

You cannot give up the truth.

You cannot give up the beautiful.

We do not throw people overboard.

We do not give up integrity.

We do not stop telling the Story that is true.

We do not duck around the hard stuff.

We evolve public culture.

We step in, turn it around, and we transform it. We do our shadow work collectively and as individuals. We actually break it open. The Hebrew word *Shever* means brokenness and is also the word that means nourishment.

Every transformation is preceded by a crisis. We want to just say it, but we do not want it to be true. We like saying that every transformation is preceded by a crisis, but we do not go through it ourselves. Instead, we say, *Let's have other people go through it, and we'll tell them how to do it.*

Then life says, *No, if you are going to lead this charge, you are going to go through it!* I'm going to go through *my breaking*. Barbara's going to go through *her breaking*. Everyone is going to go through *their breaking*.

If we are really going to be the people, and it is our turn, then we have got to go through *our breaking*.

It might be true that in the future we become beings who are attracted by the lure of becoming, and that will be enough to draw us forward. It's going to be more pull than push. But **until now, in history, there have been no major transformations that were not pushed by the pain of breaking**. In biology, in any group, there's nothing that wasn't pushed by the pain because it is risky to change! Why would we make a deep change unless we have to?

Deep jumps in evolution happen because they have to.

We are doing everything that we're doing because **life is demanding that we uplevel**. We are willing to uplevel. We are willing to stay in the pain and from the pain, move to the absolute joy, to the delight of the whole thing.

That is what we do.

That is the invitation.

APPENDIX: SONGS

THE BATTLE HYMN OF THE REPUBLIC—JULIA WARD HOWE[14]

Mine eyes have seen the glory of the coming of the Lord.

He has trampled down the vintage
  where the grapes of wrath are stored.

He has loosed the fateful lightning
  of his terrible swift sword.

His truth is marching on.

HOW COULD ANYONE—LIBBY RODERICK [15]

How could anyone ever tell you
  you were anything less than beautiful?

How could anyone ever tell you
  you were less than whole?

How could anyone fail to notice
  that your loving is a miracle—
  how deeply you're connected to my soul?

---

14   Julia Ward Howe, "The Battle Hymn of the Republic," 1862.
15   Libby Roderick, "How Could Anyone," on *If You See a Dream* (Turtle Island Records, 1990), CD.

APPENDIX: SONGS

I WANT TO KNOW WHAT LOVE IS—FOREIGNER[16]

I've gotta take a little time,
a little time to think things over.
I better read between the lines,
in case I need it when I'm older.
(Whoa, ooh-ooh, ooh-ooh)

And this mountain, I must climb
feels like the world upon my shoulders,
and through the clouds, I see love shine,
it keeps me warm as life grows colder.

[Pre-Chorus]
In my life, there's been heartache and pain.
I don't know if I can face it again.
Can't stop now, I've travelled so far
to change this lonely life.

[Chorus]
I wanna know what love is.
I want you to show me.
I wanna feel what love is.
I know you can show me.
Oh, oh-oh, oh (ooh)

I'm gonna take a little time,
a little time to look around me.
I've got nowhere left to hide,
it looks like love has finally found me.

[Pre-Chorus]

[Chorus]

[Outro]

(And I wanna feel) I wanna feel what love is

---

16 Foreigner, "I Want to Know What Love Is," recorded November 1984, on *Agent Provocateur*, Atlantic Records, vinyl LP.

(And I know) I know you can show me.
Let's talk about love.
(I wanna know what love is) The love that you feel inside.
(I want you to show me) And I'm feelin' so much love.
(I wanna feel what love is) No, you just cannot hide.
(I know you can show me) Yeah.
I wanna know what love is (Let's talk about love).
I want you to show me, I wanna feel.
(I wanna feel what love is) And I know, and I know.
I know you can show me (Yeah).
(I wanna know what love is) (I wanna know)
(I want you to show me) I wanna know, I wanna know, wanna know.
(I wanna feel what love is) (I wanna feel)
(I know you can show me).

HALLELUJAH—LEONARD COHEN[17]

Now, I've heard there was a secret chord
that David played, and it pleased the Lord.
But you don't really care for music, do you?
It goes like this, the fourth, the fifth,
the minor fall, the major lift.
The baffled king composing Hallelujah.

[Chorus]

Hallelujah, Hallelujah,
Hallelujah, Hallelujah.

Your faith was strong, but you needed proof.
You saw her bathing on the roof.
Her beauty and the moonlight overthrew you.
She tied you to a kitchen chair,
she broke your throne, and she cut your hair,
and from your lips she drew the Hallelujah.

---

17 Leonard Cohen, "Hallelujah", Various Positions, Columbia Records, 1984, LP.

[Chorus]

You say I took the name in vain,
I don't even know the name,
but if I did, well, really, what's it to you?
There's a blaze of light in every word,
it doesn't matter which you heard,
the holy or the broken Hallelujah.

[Chorus]

I did my best, it wasn't much.
I couldn't feel, so I tried to touch.
I've told the truth, I didn't come to fool you.
And even though it all went wrong,
I'll stand before the Lord of Song
With nothing on my tongue but Hallelujah.

OM NAMAH SHIVAAYA

Om Namah Shivaaya
Shivaaya namaha,
Shivaaya namah om
Shivaaya namaha, namaha Shivaaya
Shambhu Shankara namah Shivaaya,
Girijaa Shankara namah Shivaaya
Arunaachala Shiva namah Shivaaya

I bow to the soul of all. I bow to my Self. I don't know who I am, so I bow to you, Shiva, my own true Self. I bow to my teachers who loved me with love. Who took care of me when I couldn't take care of myself. I owe everything to them. How can I repay them? They have everything in the world. Only my love is mine to give, but in giving I find that it is their love flowing through me back to the world…I have nothing. I have everything. I want nothing. Only let it flow to you, my love… sing!

INDEX

Adam xii, 80
Adonai 57
alive xiii, xx, 3, 4, 13, 19, 29, 31, 32, 35, 40, 45, 51, 52, 53, 54, 55, 67, 68, 69, 76, 94, 99, 150, 151, 155
All-That-Is vii, xxviii, 10, 13, 14, 18, 22, 23, 24, 25, 64, 74, 117, 118, 123
allurement xvi, xxxv, xxxvii, 13, 14, 41, 79, 83, 145
amen 110
Amorous Cosmos 180
ananda 72
atomic 22, 96
atoms xxxvii, 2
atonement 118, 141, 142
attraction 30, 79, 83, 93
awaken xxviii, 52, 64, 67, 77, 90, 99, 106, 130, 145
aware 14, 121
awesomeness 12, 61, 94

Ba'al 77
Baal Shem Tov 77
Baruch 9, 57
beauty xxv, 12, 20, 22, 27, 31, 35, 39, 53, 66, 74, 75, 85, 86, 94, 98, 127, 129, 164, 170
Bekol 122
Bethlehem 3, 35, 54, 105, 141
Big Bang xl, xli, 11, 42, 43
biosphere 138
blood 2, 112, 113
Brahman 73, 111
brain 2, 52
breath 27, 148, 149, 157
Buber, Martin 56

Buddhism xvii, 126
bypass 58, 132

Capra, Fritjof 136, 163
certain 26, 96, 157
chai 95
Chaim 50, 51
chant 49, 53, 67, 88, 127, 146
chaos theory xvii, 26, 136
children 20, 61, 71, 86, 87, 88, 89, 134
chit 72
Christianity 14, 38, 127
circle xxvi, 26, 45, 47, 105, 135, 138, 146, 158, 162, 163
co-creator 3, 19, 64, 151
collapse xvii, xxvii, xxviii, xxxi, xxxii, xxxiii, xxxiv, 85, 161
commit 2, 43, 45, 117, 130, 154
commitment 25, 54
communion xv, xxxix, 93
community xiii, 3, 50, 77, 79
complexity xvii, 8, 22, 27, 31, 33, 44, 72, 74, 75, 136
confession 48, 100, 131
connecting 115, 135, 148, 151, 159, 160
Conscious Evolution iv, xii, xxi, xxii, 152, 153, 154, 180, 181
contraction xxvi, 65
convergence 157, 181
conversation xxii, xxix, 111, 160
CosmoErotic Humanism xii, xvi, xvii, xx, xxi, xxii, xxviii, xxxvi, xxxviii, xxxix, 101, 105, 180
Cosmos vii, xiv, xv, xvii, xx, xxvi, xxviii, xxxvi, 8, 29, 30, 32, 33,

INDEX

37, 39, 53, 54, 72, 73, 75, 76, 82, 96, 110, 111, 146, 180
creating 11, 22, 24, 53, 93, 102, 154
creation xvii, xxi, xxii, 2, 11, 13, 20, 21, 27, 28, 34, 41, 52, 53, 61, 63, 70, 71, 72, 99, 100, 107, 131, 139, 140, 141, 148, 149, 156
creativity xxv, 19, 20, 26, 27, 30, 34, 39, 40, 42, 47, 53, 60, 74, 79, 82, 100, 110, 124, 125, 131, 141, 156, 159
Creator 70, 124, 125
culture xiv, xvii, xxiii, xxv, xxx, xxxi, xxxvi, 11, 35, 41, 42, 67, 68, 74, 103, 115, 125, 145, 165, 180, 181
CWPR iv

Dante Alighieri 130
Dass, Ram 54
death xxix, xxx, xxxi, xxxvi, 16, 51
democracy 24, 35, 36, 59, 60, 61, 62, 63, 64, 66, 69, 159, 160
democratizing enlightenment xxxix, 45, 64, 109, 130, 137, 153
desire xxxiii, xxxix, 13, 20, 27, 75, 93, 95, 98, 99, 100, 101, 131
dharma xiii, 6, 60, 81, 82, 95, 98, 101, 105, 127, 142, 145, 180
dharmic 101
dignity 9, 10, 32, 33, 58, 59, 76, 98, 111, 112, 122, 128, 129, 138, 152, 155
distinction 74, 82, 83, 84, 85, 86, 109
diversity xii, xv, xxxi, xxxix, 81
divides xv, 66, 103
Divine vi, 29, 38, 39, 57, 73, 74, 75, 76, 81, 97, 101, 108, 111, 112, 118, 122, 123
dogma xiii, xiv, 115
Dowd, Michael 54

dreams 80
Earth xxvii, 3, 4, 9, 12, 21, 34, 41, 42, 66, 69, 70, 71, 80, 82, 90, 92, 111, 113, 125, 132, 138, 141, 149, 157, 163
Eckhart, Meister 38
ecstasy 39, 57, 65, 75, 97, 98, 132
ecstatic xiii, 3, 42, 69, 108, 109, 112, 136, 155
ego 14, 24, 36, 45, 46, 66, 76, 77, 82, 84, 90, 103, 138
egocentric 16, 45
Egypt 21
electromagnetic 95
electron 19, 70, 79
Eliade, Mircea 161
Eloheinu 57
embodied iv
emerge xix, 56, 64, 82
empower xviii
enlightenment xxxix, 45, 64, 109, 130, 137, 153
epiphanies 8, 15
Erhard, Werner 64
Eros xvi, xvii, xviii, xxi, xxvi, xxvii, xxviii, xxxiii, xxxv, xxxvii, 55, 65, 72, 83, 84, 95, 130, 163, 180
  impulse 7
  Intimacy 7
  Love 13
  partners xiii
  relationship 2
  spirituality 55
  Story 60
  Unique Self 61
Essential Self 98
ethnocentric xiv, 112, 120
evolution xiv, xv, xvii, xxi, xxii, xxiv, xxv, xxvi, xxx, xxxvi, xxxviii, xxxix, xl, xli, 6, 7, 8, 11, 12, 13, 14, 19, 20, 21, 24, 27, 28,

34, 41, 42, 48, 52, 53, 54, 55,
  57, 60, 61, 63, 67, 68, 69, 73,
  74, 76, 81, 91, 96, 98, 99, 101,
  102, 105, 106, 108, 112, 113,
  116, 123, 128, 131, 132, 134,
  137, 139, 140, 145, 153, 156,
  157, 160, 163, 165, 181
 of intimacy 121
 of love 123
Evolutionary vi, vii, viii, xii, xiii, xix,
  xx, xxii, 13, 18, 19, 20, 21, 22,
  23, 24, 25, 27, 30, 34, 36, 40,
  49, 60, 63, 66, 67, 68, 69, 70,
  71, 72, 73, 74, 82, 83, 84, 85,
  89, 90, 91, 93, 98, 107, 108,
  110, 130, 131, 132, 135, 137,
  139, 140, 141, 145, 152, 154,
  155, 158, 163, 180
 Church 141
Evolutionary Love vi, viii, xiii, xix,
  xxii, 13, 18, 19, 20, 21, 22, 23,
  24, 25, 27, 34, 36, 40, 49, 63,
  66, 67, 69, 70, 71, 72, 74, 83,
  84, 89, 91, 93, 107, 108, 130,
  132, 135, 163, 180
existential risk xxv, xxix, xxx, xxxiii,
  xxxiv, xxxv, xxxvi, xxxvii,
  xxxviii, 150, 151, 153, 154,
  162
Eye 2, 30, 37, 40, 42, 59, 74, 87, 92,
  168
 of Humanity 41
 of Spirit 114
 of Value 180

faith 132, 161, 170
Farrell, Warren 96
features xix
feelings xxxv, xxxvi, 4, 17, 27, 53,
  67, 77, 92, 97, 106, 107, 108,
  109, 111, 112, 113, 114, 115,
  116, 125, 126, 134, 135, 140,
  146, 149

feminine 156
feminism 161
Feuerbach, Ludwig 14
First Principles iii, xiv, xv, xvi, xx,
  xxii, xxiv, xxv, xxviii, xxix,
  xxxi, xxxiv, xxxviii, 180, 181
forgive 118
freedom 12, 19, 27, 53, 61, 69, 98,
  108, 131
fulfilment 34, 75, 98, 99, 100
fundamental 44
fundamentalism 37, 76
fundamentalist xx, 32, 39, 75, 76,
  97, 109, 112, 120, 121

Gafni, Marc xvii, 180, 181
gender 96
genes xxii, 93, 100, 101
genius xxii, 11, 34, 53, 62, 63, 64,
  67, 70, 75, 93, 100, 101, 124,
  156, 159
gifts xviii, xxiii, 42, 47, 64, 126, 131
Global viii, xxxiv, xxxvi, xxxviii, 92,
  181
 ethos xv
 intimacy xvii
Goddess 39, 75
God Self 149
gorgeousness 13, 31, 74, 77, 94, 98,
  145
Gospel 55
ground xiii, xiv, xv, xxix, xxxix, 88,
  143, 180

haKadosh Baruch Hu 9
hallel 38, 59
Hallelujah 31, 32, 38, 48, 50, 51, 55,
  58, 59, 75, 76, 84, 97, 112,
  122, 132, 137, 138, 154, 155,
  156, 160, 164, 170, 171
Hasidic 49
Hebrew 57, 59, 95, 120, 122, 126,
  165
hero 5

INDEX

hierarchy 82, 99, 100, 103
holelut 59, 112, 122
Homo amor xiii, xxi, 93
Homo sapiens xiii, 139, 180
Homo sapiens sapiens xiii, 139, 180
Homo universalis 2
Hubbard, Barbara Marx iii, iv, xii, 65, 67, 180, 181
human xvii, xxi, xxvii, xxviii, xxix, xxx, xxxi, xxxii, xxxiii, xxxv, xxxvii, xxxix, xl, 1, 2, 3, 11, 13, 14, 20, 21, 26, 29, 34, 35, 37, 51, 62, 64, 67, 78, 83, 91, 93, 99, 102, 103, 130, 139, 152, 164, 180
humanity xiii, xvi, xviii, xxii, xxx, xxxi, xl, xli, 2, 12, 13, 20, 41, 93, 99, 101, 113, 115, 133, 141, 148, 160, 180, 181
humans 2, 3, 11, 17, 20, 67, 70, 78, 102, 157

identity xv, xxxiii, xxxv, xxxvi, xxxvii, xxxix, 180
illusion 91, 116, 126, 128
imagination 10, 14, 31, 74, 75
imagine 10, 30, 31, 42, 74, 92, 96, 110, 134, 139, 140, 141, 154, 156, 164
individual xiv, xxvii, xxxvii, 51, 59, 60, 61, 63
individuals xxxi, 63, 165
Infinity of Intimacy viii, xx, xxi, 7, 8, 9, 10, 29, 37, 57, 58, 59, 75, 92, 97, 111, 112, 121, 123, 137, 149
Infinity of Power xx, 7, 29, 30, 57, 75, 121, 137
influence xxvi, 26, 45, 47
Inside of the Inside 72, 73
integral 109
Integral Theory 64
integrity xix, 5, 68, 86, 164, 165

intimacy xvii, xxvi, xxviii, xxxiii, xxxiv, xxxv, xxxvi, xxxvii, xxxviii, xli, 10, 14, 17, 18, 22, 23, 26, 29, 37, 45, 47, 55, 57, 92, 93, 94, 98, 99, 100, 101, 102, 103, 104, 106, 107, 108, 109, 110, 111, 112, 115, 117, 118, 121, 122, 123, 126, 129, 134, 135, 136, 137, 138, 145, 146, 148, 149
Intimate Universe ix, xxi, xxxvi, 14, 15, 102, 111, 121, 123, 135, 136, 137, 142, 145, 146

Jantsch, Erich 163
Jerusalem 3, 54, 105
Jesus 1, 2, 3, 9, 11, 15, 47, 80, 97, 110
joining genes xxii, 100
joining genius xxii, 93, 100, 156, 159
Kabbalah xvii, 38, 113, 180
Kant, Immanuel 120
Karov 110
Kashmir Shaivism xvii, 38, 53
Kauffman, Stuart 110
Kempton, Sally xii, 122
kensho 130
kinderlach 88
king 95, 143, 144, 170
kiss 96, 97, 114
Kodesh 73
Kook, Abraham 56
Krishna 54, 59
Kurzweil, Arthur 89
Kurzweil, Ray 152

leaders xii, 103, 159
leadership xii, 103
leading xv, xxi, 64, 79, 140, 180
Lechisha 15, 110
line 11, 162
loneliness 36, 75, 99, 148, 149, 150
longing 98, 100

Love vi, vii, viii, ix, x, xiii, xix, xxii, xxiv, xxvii, xxxii, xxxvi, xxxix, 13, 14, 18, 19, 20, 21, 22, 23, 24, 25, 27, 29, 30, 34, 36, 40, 43, 44, 45, 48, 49, 60, 63, 66, 67, 68, 69, 70, 71, 72, 73, 74, 77, 78, 80, 81, 82, 83, 84, 85, 86, 87, 89, 90, 91, 93, 95, 104, 106, 107, 108, 112, 114, 119, 120, 126, 127, 128, 129, 130, 132, 135, 138, 140, 145, 147, 154, 163, 169, 180
LoveIntelligence xxvi, 13, 18, 24, 27, 29, 37, 39, 47, 59, 97, 111, 145, 150

Mackey, John xii
masculine 156
mathematics 37, 75
matrix xxxiv, 180
meditation 27, 28, 30, 107, 108
melech 57, 95
memetic 153
memory xxxvi, xxxviii, 20, 52, 53, 144, 163, 164
memory of the future xxxvi, 20, 52, 144, 163, 164
miracle 2, 15, 97, 100, 103, 168
modern xv, xvii, xxvii, xxxv, xxxvii, xxxix, 96, 120
modernity xxxii, xxxiii, 6
molecule 2, 52
mother 72, 73, 114, 116, 150, 155
Murphy, Michael 6
music xix, 44, 61, 86, 170
mystica 111
mysticism 73, 118

Naam, Ramez 151
Nachman of Breslov 142
namah 147, 171
New Age 13, 129, 153, 155, 164
new human 1, 2, 3, 11, 35, 93, 180
new humanity xiii, 93, 101, 180

noosphere 12, 14, 63

obligation 73
olam 57
OLATT 119
Outrageous Acts of Love 43, 45, 126, 130, 154
Outrageous Love vii, viii, ix, xiii, xix, xxii, xxvii, xxxix, 13, 14, 18, 24, 29, 30, 43, 66, 68, 70, 71, 72, 73, 74, 78, 80, 81, 82, 83, 84, 85, 86, 87, 89, 90, 91, 95, 106, 119, 127, 129, 130, 145
Outrageous Love Story xxxix, 13

Pentecost xxii, 79, 80, 81
pleasure 83, 84, 85, 153
pointing-out instruction 93
postmodern xv, xxxix, 5, 6
power xviii, xxviii, xxxiii, xxxix, 5, 8, 29, 30, 31, 35, 36, 37, 41, 47, 48, 59, 70, 74, 85, 98, 111, 112, 121, 151, 156
prayer xix, xx, 4, 6, 8, 9, 10, 28, 32, 33, 35, 36, 37, 53, 55, 56, 57, 58, 60, 67, 76, 77, 80, 96, 97, 104, 108, 110, 111, 112, 114, 120, 122, 123, 126, 128, 135, 136, 137, 138, 155
premodern xv, 5, 39
promise 2
prophet 10
proton 19, 70, 79
psychology xxvii, 96, 150
purpose xxxv, xxxvi, 19, 20, 21, 93, 99, 117

quantum 81, 157, 181

Rachmana 9
Rama 38, 59
Ramakrishna 39, 137
Reality vii, ix, x, xiv, xvii, xx, xxi,

INDEX

xxv, xxviii, xxxiii, xxxv, xxxvii, xxxviii, xxxix, xl, xli, 7, 8, 9, 12, 13, 14, 22, 24, 28, 29, 30, 31, 37, 38, 44, 47, 51, 56, 65, 68, 73, 75, 83, 97, 110, 111, 120, 121, 122, 123, 128, 130, 135, 136, 137, 163
realization xiv, xvii, xx, xxi, xxviii, xxix, xxx, xxxviii, 21, 44, 58, 135, 136, 137
relationship 2, 29, 121, 152
religion xxxii, xxxix, 14, 75, 80, 81, 105, 115, 124, 142, 180
Renaissance xxiv, xxxi, 55, 152, 153
repulsion 30
resonance xxxiv, 4, 34, 53, 56, 93, 95, 96, 102, 141, 160
revelation 107
Rumi xxvi, 30, 32, 37, 38, 56, 96

sacred xli, 12, 34, 46, 52, 53, 60, 81, 83, 95, 102, 110, 118, 126, 127
sangha 4, 67, 103, 141, 147
sat-chit-ananda 72
security 99
self-organizing 2, 13, 25, 26, 27, 44, 47, 51
sensemaking xiv, xx, xxi, xxvi, xxxiii, xxxv, xxxvii, 24, 34, 38, 43, 54, 60, 108, 124, 130, 135, 136, 148
separate self 44, 65
separation 44, 80, 91, 113, 116, 134, 135, 148
sex 76, 77
sexing 77
sexual 77, 93, 130
sexuality 77, 93, 130
shadow 165
Shakta 73
Shakti 38, 73, 111
shivaya 146
Source ix, 11, 19, 55, 73, 86, 148, 149
source code xvii, xxiii, xxv, 44, 101, 110, 153, 180, 181
Spirit 7, 28, 37, 80, 96, 98, 114, 115, 155, 159, 160, 161
Stein, Zachary xxix, 180
story xxi, xxv, xxxii, xxxiii, xxxiv, xxxv, xxxvii, xxxviii, xxxix, xl, xli, 2, 6, 7, 11, 12, 13, 14, 16, 21, 24, 34, 49, 53, 57, 60, 63, 65, 81, 86, 88, 95, 105, 124, 130, 131, 142, 143, 144, 150, 152, 153, 155, 160, 161, 162, 163, 164, 180

Tagore, Rabindranath 83
telerotic xxii, 153
Telerotic Universe 153
temple 21, 117
tenderness 109, 112
the whole xv, xxiii, xxiv, 2, 5, 7, 24, 34, 36, 42, 43, 46, 53, 67, 71, 98, 99, 100, 105, 107, 113, 114, 123, 125, 126, 129, 130, 143, 146, 149, 150, 151, 152, 154, 158, 166
Thou Art That 109
traditions xiii, xiv, xvii, xxi, 29, 35, 37, 38, 74, 109, 121, 129, 132
tragic xiii, 33, 126
transformation 162, 165
tribe 146
True Self 128
truth xxv, xxvii, xxxix, 6, 10, 15, 40, 77, 136, 151, 159, 164, 168, 171
Turing, Alan 25, 44
Tzaratam 122

umka 73
understanding xviii, xl, 52, 53, 55
unio xxxvi, 65, 93, 99, 148
unique gift 13, 14, 18, 22, 23, 26, 41, 45, 47, 66, 125, 140, 145, 154

uniqueness xv, 22, 23, 135, 142, 143
Unique Self vi, vii, ix, xiii, xvi, xvii, xxi, xxii, xli, 2, 4, 12, 13, 18, 20, 21, 22, 23, 24, 25, 26, 27, 36, 41, 42, 43, 44, 45, 46, 48, 49, 51, 61, 64, 65, 66, 68, 81, 98, 99, 100, 102, 107, 115, 130, 134, 135, 139, 140, 141, 142, 143, 144, 145, 146, 147, 149, 153, 154, 160, 180
Unique Self Symphony ix, xvii, xli, 2, 4, 13, 20, 25, 26, 27, 36, 41, 42, 43, 44, 45, 46, 48, 49, 51, 64, 65, 66, 81, 102, 115, 141, 142, 143, 144, 147, 149, 153, 154, 160
unique voice 102
Universe vi, ix, x, xiv, xv, xxi, xxii, xxix, xxxii, xxxiii, xxxvi, xli, 6, 11, 13, 14, 15, 17, 19, 21, 25, 26, 27, 28, 41, 42, 48, 70, 71, 73, 74, 99, 102, 111, 112, 121, 123, 124, 135, 136, 137, 142, 145, 146, 152, 153, 163
Universe Story x, xv, xxxii, xxxiii, 6, 21, 152, 153

values xiii, xiv, xxxiii, xxxiv, xxxvii, xxxviii, 6, 44, 161

vocational arousal xxii, 62

Walden 9, 111
WeSpace 61
Wheel of Co-Creation vii, 61, 62, 64, 151, 181
where we are 16, 35, 43, 143
who we are 109
Wilber, Ken xii, xvi, 136, 181
wisdom xiii, xv, xvii, xxi, xl, 33, 59, 126
World War II 25, 86, 161

xenophobic 5, 32, 75, 97

yearning 19, 20, 27, 33, 61, 62, 67, 69, 72, 75, 88, 92, 93, 100, 101, 140, 150

Zohar 15

ABOUT THE AUTHORS

Dr. Marc Gafni is a visionary world philosopher and futurist, one of the leading formulators of world spirituality and religion of our time, and a beloved teacher and public intellectual. He holds his doctorate in philosophy from Oxford University, as well as Orthodox rabbinic ordination. He co-founded the activist think tank, now called the Center for World Philosophy and Religion where he serves as the co-president with Dr. Zachary Stein. He also served with Barbara Marx Hubbard as co-president of the Foundation for Conscious Evolution, which he consented to lead at Barbara's request after her passing.

He is known for his "source code teachings"—including Unique Self theory and the Five Selves, the Amorous Cosmos, a Politics of Evolutionary Love, a Return to Eros, and Digital Intimacy—and has more than twenty books to his name, including the award-winning Your Unique Self, A Return to Eros, and three volumes of Radical Kabbalah.

He teaches on the cutting edge of philosophy in the West, helping to evolve a new "dharma" or meta-theory of Integral meaning that is helping to reshape key pivoting points in global consciousness and culture, with the aim of participating in the articulation of what Dr. Gafni together with Dr. Stein and colleagues are calling CosmoErotic Humanism.

At the core of CosmoErotic Humanism is what Dr. Gafni and Dr. Stein are calling First Principles and First Values, Anthro-Ontology, and a Universal Grammar of Value. This is the ground of a new shared universe story and a new narrative of identity for the new human and the new humanity. This is what they are calling the emergence from Homo sapiens to Homo Amor. This shared story rooted in First Principles and First Values can then serve as the matrix for a global ethos for a global civilization.

Together with Dr. Stein and Ken Wilber, Gafni is writing a series of seminal books under the collective pseudonym of David J. Temple, which intend to evolve the source code of consciousness and culture in response to the meta-crisis. The first of those books is *First Principles and First Values: Forty-Two Propositions on CosmoErotic Humanism, the Meta-Crisis, and the World to Come*.

Barbara Marx Hubbard (born Barbara Marx; December 22, 1929–April 10, 2019) was an American futurist, author, and public speaker. She is credited with the Wheel of Co-Creation and together with Dr. Gafni, the Wheel of Co-Creation 2.0, as well as the concepts of the Synergy Engine and the "birthing" of humanity.

As co-founder and president of the Foundation for Conscious Evolution and the chair, for the last five years of her life, of the Center for World Philosophy and Religion, she posited that humanity was on the threshold of a quantum leap if newly emergent scientific, social, and spiritual capacities were integrated to address global crises.

She was the author of seven books on social and planetary evolution. In conjunction with the Shift Network, she co-produced the worldwide "Birth 2012" multimedia event. She was also the subject of a biography by author Neale Donald Walsch, *The Mother of Invention: The Legacy of Barbara Marx Hubbard*. Deepak Chopra called her "the voice for conscious evolution."

In 1984, she was symbolically nominated for the vice presidency of the United States. She also co-chaired a number of Soviet-American Citizen Summits, introducing a new concept called SYNCON, to foster synergistic convergence with opposing groups. In addition, she co-founded the World Future Society and the Association for Global New Thought.

Volume 2 — Healing The Global Intimacy Disorder

LIST OF EPISODES

1. Episode 11 — January 7, 2017
2. Episode 12 — January 14, 2017
3. Episode 13 — January 20, 2017
4. Episode 14 — January 28, 2017
5. Episode 15 — February 4, 2017
6. Episode 16 — February 11, 2017
7. Episode 17 — February 18, 2017
8. Episode 18 — February 25, 2017
9. Episode 19 — March 4, 2017
10. Episode 20 — March 11, 2017

www.ingramcontent.com/pod-product-compliance
Lightning Source LLC
LaVergne TN
LVHW011153080426
835508LV00007B/376